Praise for
Waiting on the Monsoons for His Desert Soul

    Reading RedWulf DancingBare's poetry shines a light into all the dark places in my heart and soul, illuminating those things I'm afraid to look at. I know no means of processing those in the deft way RedWulf is able. Without instruction, with no effort, when I read RedWulf's work, I feel immersed in a psychic hot spring, engulfed suddenly, comforted, enveloped, understood, as I KNOW I am because his poetry speaks my heart. In ways and with words I could never conjure. I'm exposed and protected all at once. Seen and embraced. RedWulf knows these feelings, but also knows how to navigate and shape them into a form that can be applied like a healing salve. I adore his work; every word I have ever read has left me dumbfounded at his ability to clarify human experience at its most raw, and in his hands it becomes like a gem, so many facets, such beauty, a wonderment.

    What can I say to a person holding this book in their hands, considering spending time with it — Oh, DO!! Do, and then you will, over and over again. And every time you read these words, you will come away with a new flavor, a new understanding, a deeper appreciation for a being who can shine a light on what so many of us feel, but cannot express.

Christine Scheurich

Waiting on the Monsoons for His Desert Soul

Text and Photographs by

RedWulf DancingBare

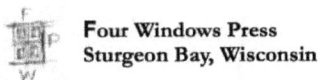
Four Windows Press
Sturgeon Bay, Wisconsin

Copyright © 2020 by Ralph Victor Greco

All rights reserved. No part of this publication may be reproduced, distributed or transmitted in any form or by any means, without prior written permission.

Ralph Victor Greco/Four Windows Press
231 North Hudson
Sturgeon Bay, WI 54235
www.fourwindowspress1.com

Publisher's Note: This is a work of poetry. Names, characters, places, and incidents are a product of the author's life and imagination. Locales and public names are sometimes used for atmospheric purposes. Any resemblance to actual people, living or dead, or to businesses, companies, events, institutions, or locales is completely coincidental.

Book Layout © 2017 BookDesignTemplates.com

Waiting on the Monsoons for His Desert Soul, Redwulf Dancingbare. -- 1st ed.

ISBN: 978-0-9990077-3-0

This book can be ordered from the Galleria Carnaval Gallery at http:galleriacarnaval.com, 4018 Ice Caves Road, NM 53, Mile Marker 46, El Morro, NM 87321. All Four Windows Press books can be ordered through the gallery.

Dedication

This book is dedicated to all two-spirited children who have yet to find their unique voice, their sense of truth, and the authentic creativity of their lives. May this book inspire you to live a little more wildly and a little more freely. May it call to you to find a way to explore new landscapes (internal and external), and to seek out soul adventures. May it call you to allow yourself to heed the intuitive voice within you, and to find your "Two Spirit" balance needed. For I believe that we two spirits are the way-showers and the healers for the rigid thinking, and the fall-in-line stuck-ness that the world will continue to endure in the cause of just being safe (but not really alive or in balance). Dream! Dare! Delve!

Love, RedWulf DancingBare

Acknowledgements

I wish to thank Tom Davis (*The Weirding Storm*) for believing in me long before I believed in myself, and for helping me to create, edit, and publish this book. I am forever grateful!

I wish to thank Standing Feather, my amazing partner of 13 years, for living this dream with me, for believing in my words and honoring my soul, and for giving me the safety, security, and love needed to materialize a lifetime desire to be a writer.

I wish to thank The Zuni Mountain Poets, who for the last 18 years have kept the sacred ground for a weekly Sunday Poetry group that has affirmed me, uplifted me, and inspired me. Special thanks to Jack North for being a guiding star for me and for this group.

I wish to thank countless family and friends who have inspired and loved me, particularly: Deb, Mick, Diane, Dan, Christine, Tonii, my beautiful family, Feather's wonderful family, Elkkin, Penny, John, Tom, Tom and Ethel, Dana, James, Marge, Paula, Sharron, Melani, and…

The following poems have been published in the following places:

Another Trojan War," *Zuni Mountain Poets,* John Carter North, Margaret Gross, and Thomas Davis editors. 2012. (Bloomington, IN: iUniverse, Inc.), pp. 121-122.

"Death by Pink," *Zuni Mountain Poets,* John Carter North, Margaret Gross, and Thomas Davis editors. 2012. (Bloomington, IN: iUniverse, Inc.), pp.118-119.

"A Jealous Wind," *Querencia,* John Carter North editor.2014. (A Mini Anthology of Poems), originally titled "Wind Fall", pp.28

"Christmas Eve Mastications," Face Book,12/24/19

"Witch Hunt, The Real Thing," Face Book, 10/6/19

"On the Wire," Face Book, 9/1/19

"Waiting on the Monsoons for His Desert Soul," Face Book, 6/30/19

"White Winkte' Day," Face Book, 6/7/19

"Just Walking My Path," Face Book', 5/12/19

"A Dark Night of His Soul," Face Book, 3/31/19

"In the Desert," Face Book, 3/24/19

"Where Do You Place Your Burden Basket," Face Book, 1/13/19
"Earth Roots," Face Book, 12/22/18
"The Art of Human Being," Face Book, 12/16/18
"Do You Sing In Your Cage?" Face Book, 11/18/18
"Empire of the Son," Face Book, 10/28/18
"Know Your Bones," Face Book, 10/7/18
"Once a Clown," Face Book, 9/30/18
"Whale Songs," Face Book, 7/22/18
"Free at Last," Face Book, 7/8/18
"Just a Tiny Teacup," Face Book, 6/17/18
"For the People," Face Book, 4/15/18
"Earth Day, 1970," face Book, 3/25/18
"Two Spirit Dancing," Face Book, 2/11/18
"The Dragon Within," Face Book, 1/14/18
"When the First Door opened," Face Book, 12/3/17
"Magdalena De Luz," Face Book, 11/12/17
"The Show Must Go On, But Wait!", Face Book, 10/15/17
"Up the Stairs," Face Book, 10/1/17
"Happy Father's Day," Face Book, 6/11/17
"Grace," Face Book, 5/29/17

Table of Contents

INTRODUCTION iii
Up the Stairs 3
A Ritual of Heathens 4
Earth Roots 7
Mithra Deis Natalis Sol Invicti 8
Solstice Devotion 10
Inevitable Processions 12
For Donald Sharp 13
Coal Chiseling Diamonds 15
Grace 17
The Art of Human Being 20
To The Table 22
No Poem Today 23
Some Man's Garden 25
Full Athena 27
Magdalena de Luz 28
Secret Ingredients 30
Polar Shifts 32
If It Takes A Village 33
Earth Day 35
Evolution 36
Will I Find You in the Wilderness? 37
Punks 39
Neptune's Lover 43
Illegitimi Non Carborundum! 47

Numbered Days 49

The Box 53

The River And The Stone 55

Tree Rings 57

Harbor Waves 59

In the Desert 61

Caw of the Wild 63

Christmas Eve Mastications 64

Prophesied 66

Under the Gypsy Moon 67

The Ritual 70

The Last Performance 74

Metal 77

Empty Box Karma 79

Captain 80

The Seasons 82

Empire of the Son 85

A Mote of God's Eye 87

The Earth, the Fire, the Water, ... 90

the Air, Return, Return, Return, Return! 90

A Dark Night of His Soul 93

A Jealous Wind 94

Another Trojan War 96

Dem Bones, Dem Bones, ... 98

Dem Dry Bones 98

On the Threshold 100

On the Wire 102

The Baker	104
The River	106
The Formative Years	110
He Didn't See That Coming!	112
Your Children	115
The Bittersweet Sound	118
of Old Trains Whistling By	118
In Training	123
Happy Father's Day	125
Death By Pink	129
Disciplined Wild One	131
Free At Last	133
Rocket Man	137
When the First Door Opened	141
Once a Clown	147
The Show Must Go On! But Wait!	151
Whale Songs	154
A Most Hate Filled Name	157
Among the Sacred Sun Drops	159
Sanctuary	162
For the People	165
Two Spirit Dancing	170
White Winkte' Day	174
The Potter	179
Just a Tiny Teacup	182
Nature of Things	185
Do You Sing In Your Cage?	189

The Culling Times 192
"Witch Hunt, the Real Thing" 196
Know Your Bones 199
The Hand Me Down Bullet 202
(Or Man's Eternal Hernia) 202
Waiting on the Monsoons 204
for His Desert Soul 204
Where Do You Place Your 207
Burden Basket 207
Just Walking My Path 211
Redwulf Dancingbare 217

INTRODUCTION

The first time I saw Redwulf he was leading a group of gay men on a trance-drum journey to meet our ancestral spirit guides. It was early summer 2007 and I, by a small miracle, had arrived at Zuni Mountain Sanctuary in New Mexico for a one week 'Shaman's Gathering' with a shattered life and a terrible cocaine addiction. During his workshop, the tempo and song of the drum felt ancient to my body. The results were profoundly effective. I learned during the post-journey discussion that the same soothing pulse and poetic rhythms were present when he spoke. I formed an instant love and admiration for a man that I had never met before, but whose words were suddenly healing the connective-tissues of my confused and injured psyche.

The poems in Waiting on the Monsoons for His Desert Soul showcase a love for language and a desire to offer words that ease the agonies of vulnerability and human suffering. They are a master storyteller's collection of the elemental reconciliations of the human mind, body, and spirit. Laced throughout the poems are surprisingly unique, sometimes gritty, and often humorous instances of seemingly everything we can experience in life, from the immense pleasures to the unimaginable sorrows. Weaved throughout are peeks into Redwulf's remarkable life, including poems offering boundless wisdom resulting from stints as a circus clown, steward of a radical faerie sanctuary, Unitarian Universalist Lay-Minister, a Lakota Sundancer, and an accomplished chef and baker.

The centerpiece to many of the poems is the relationship between different aspects inside the body when saturated with the many contradictions the world presents. The tension between Thought, Will, Heart Emotions, and the Physical Body is brilliantly on display. Additionally, each poem manages to peek into the mysterious realm between the mundane and the ethereal:

In his small village,
The people were the balm of God.
The people shared their tears like manna from heaven,
so that each and every one was fed and comforted.

The many stories within this book dive deeply into the possibilities that arise from both uncertainty and hope. Again and again, the reader is left to draw similarities and resolutions to their own lives. The poems are an invitation for the reader to view a panorama landscape of their soul. Despite the magnitude of personal struggle presented here, Redwulf leads us to a hard-fought salvation. He has created a guidebook to making allies out of the limiting characteristics that keep one from manifesting their highest potential. In his healing practice, he teaches the ancient concept of being a "walks-between," a traveler of both the external and internal worlds, the physical and spiritual, the male and the female. For Redwulf life is a multi-colored palate that skews the lines of polarization. In his view, the separation we create between ourselves and the universe, god, our ancestors and so on is simply a lack of remembering. The poems beckon humanity to operate with boundless love at the center of their medicine wheel:

> She could feel her inner dragon
> flexing once majestic wings of grace,
> now struggling stubs.
> Its tears would flood in torrents
> and then seep into her cracked slit beseechings,
> karmically cocooned in senseless sarcophagi.
> The weavings of her fear
> and the warpings of her shame unraveled
> to reveal her humanities struggle.
> And her dragon inside would rejoice
> for the remembrance of forgiveness.

Words like remembrance and forgiveness are the foundations that help the reader to stand up against the cold blowing winds of self-doubt resulting from trauma. Illuminated throughout the book are small beacons of light intended to bring serenity to people that are healing childhood wounds related to abuse and neglect. His honest accounts of his own childhood draw us back into the pains of not feeling heard, not feeling seen, and not feeling honored for our inherent ideological truths. The wisdom inside the poetry reminds us that we can attempt to transmute poisons and transform limitations by thanking them directly before releasing them back into the earth to be rejuvenated into life force energy:

> When puberty came
> with unshod dread he began to tread
> the mined-fields and booby-trapped farm
> of his fomenting father and uncle.
> He quickly grew wary of the psychic trip wires
> that could suddenly blast forth in bombastic harangue.
> He despised the blistering belittlement bombs that
> scorched all in hot foot range,
> But that especially seemed to target him.
>
> He grows with tender feet.

And later in the poem:

> Less victimized are his feet now – taking responsibility for much more of his own causations
> and understanding abandonment can be a pre-chosen shoe insertion.
> Less running away are his own feet now – willing to more face the two left-footed times,
> and the ungrounded feet-over-his-head times,
>
> and the feet in the same-rut boring times,
> as well as the feet-don't-fail-me-now times.
> Less unhappy are his feet now – from not stopping his own dreams afoot
> and following them to their own perfectly imperfect walkabouts
> regardless of whether they were "success or disasters"
> according to other people's reality footholds.
>
> They are his own still tender two feet.

Certainly, his love for unique sentence structure and uses of alliteration and word-scrambling are a unique and delightful experience for the reader. Redwulf honed his writing skills during his many years as member of the Zuni Mountain Poets group in El Morro, New Mexico. The freedom allowed in the group to express himself poetically allowed for Redwulf himself to explore and find elements of healing needed in his own life. In addition, the weekly exposure to accomplished poets such as Ethel Davis, Paula Sayword and James Janko deepened his understanding of how the poem begins to inhale and exhale its own life and vitality. As fellow Zuni Mountain Poet Ward O'Cean writes of Redwulf's poetry:

> His clickety-clackety syllabic constructs
> Chase us into the hidden pathways and bridges
> Deep inside our own story.

Standing Feather
El Morro, New Mexico

BOOK I

REMEMBRANCES, PRAYERS, SEASONAL DEDICATIONS, AND DITTIES

Up the Stairs

Up the stairs is a procession.
    We each climb one rise at a time. We each follow another.
    We are each followed by another, not in the locking of our steps, but
    in the stretching of our souls.

Up the stairs
    is a pilgrimage in honoring the poetry of ever-changing mystery:
    as we listen to the heartbeat of the riser,
    as we charge ourselves in the cadence of the pacer, as we reflect our
        own baggage
    against the weight being carried by those who are climbing.

Up the stairs one lifting at a time,
    a foot, a word, a reason, a rhyme,
    bridging the levels,
    each never at the place they were before.

    What place have they come to now?
    What is the feeling of the beauty they behold?
    What is the power of the fire that propels?
    What is the color of the audacity in their passion?
    What is the beat of the courage in their poetic justice?

It is in the act of climbing that the poem is created.
Up the stairs is the synergy of heart with art,
up the many steps raising feet, lifting spirit.

Hold on loosely to the railing!
    It can be a guide and a safety,
    or a restriction and a curse.
    The people below laugh and gossip, unaware,
    while the spark of evolution and revolution
    kindles and courses in the choir loft,
    resounding the sacred voices of each step.

Based on climbing stairs each Sunday morning to join the Zuni Mountain Poets' sanctuary.

A Ritual of Heathens

The ground elk, cranberries, hickory nuts, and egg yolks
squished through her small hands like Play Dough.
A giggle escaped as if through a steam valve opening.
She clamped down on it quickly,
whipping her head side to side to see who might be watching.

"Aunt Esther would have been yelling at me by now
for playing with the soul cakes," she echoed to herself.
The former, momentary, elation quickly overtaken
by the feeling of loss of her beloved aunt.

She patted out each of the six patties.
"There, one for John, sweet, sweet boy,"
shaking her head with a faraway smile.
"One for Tommy," she said with a grimace,
then a shrug of acceptance.
"One for Mark's mom,
one for poor rich Ol' Mrs Courtney,
and one for Aunt Esther," a tear escaping the corral of her eye
that she shepherded quickly onto her handkerchief.
"And then one for all the rest who have passed this year."

She laid the neat round embodiments out in a line
and sprinkled salt lightly on each patty's face.
"Salt to honor your blood's coursing,
salt to cleanse your holdings pain,
salt to pay you for your teachings,
salt to lead you home again."
The invocation chanted as the old family rote coursed.

Then she sprinkled thyme on each.
"A sweet and gentle passage on you,
each and every blessed soul;
thyme make your hearts forgiving

and your spirits once more whole."

She thought about Tommy and her dad
always at one another's throats.
They would bellow and snort at each other
like two elk stags she had watched fighting,
locking horns and threatening to take out
almost every dinner table at which they sat together.
She threw a little extra thyme on Tommy's,
blew a thyme dervish into the air to her father—
wherever he might be.

She continued,
"Onion powder to remember what you shed,
a little pepper to recall what gave you mission,
some garlic to remember patient sweetness
and honor where you took your visions."
Finally, she sprinkled sage on them each.
"Love honored as eternal,
this life's journey just one kiss,
sage to help release you
from what you think you couldn't miss."

Her mother's joke
that she bet Ol' Mrs. Courtney had all her servants
put to death, embalmed, and put in her mausoleum with her casket,
made her shake her head at the thought
of one being so ornery and greedy.
Or was Mrs. Courtney just in too much pain? She wondered.
She remembered how she didn't even seem to be able
to butter toast for herself.
"How could one so dependent not be close enough
to see the aching pain in others?" she said to herself.
She lit some piled sage on the mantle
and let its gentle blanket soothe her unquiet.

She fried the cherished healing cakes up in butter and oil.
"Well, a little fat is not going to hurt you now,

is it Sweet John?"
She remembered the young neighbor boy so large
that his parents had to cut a larger front door on their house
because he had to work to get through the regular one.
She thought of the slow-minded boy
joyfully feeding squirrels peanuts in their yard,
his excitement and zeal squeals
that stopped the squirrels in their tracks,
but didn't keep them from the nuts.

She smiled, envisioning him floating lighter than air,
now able to look at the "birdies" in the treetop nests
that seemed to obsess him.

She fixed each one a plate full.
She gave them each a soul cake on a buttermilk biscuit,
except John's on a white flour tortilla,
a potato salad scoop, and 2 apple quarters,
and a pile of steaming bitter greens with oil and vinegar and lemon.
She put on some special imported Greek figs just for Aunt Esther.
She arranged them on the table by the fireplace
at the head of all the other tables,
then lit all the candles in the great welcoming room.
She made sure everything was ready to receive the Samhain guests,
especially this year's passing ones,
so they could all dine and dance together for the next three days
as they said their God-Speeds and bon voyages.
Then each could start the fresh new year
with fewer bones rattling in their closets.

Earth Roots

On this shortest day of light,
call upon your remembrance of the regal sunflower
if the fear within the darkness threatens to overtake you.
For the sunflower seed in its winter bed
has welcomed the cold and the dark to crystallize its mission.
Let it impart unto you its natural trust
that the increasing light
will again spur it to its fullest glory,
to tower against azure summer skies
and gladden the hearts of all who witness.
And if your soul feels exhausted,
and your body aches with drudgery,
call upon this earth
to be the womb of your next self re-creation.
Rest with your inner seed safe and nurtured.
Dream and imagine your inner blossom
already strong and bright and ready for gifting.
And if you seem to lose your way and feel ungrounded,
call upon the cold, full moon to illumine your psyche
in a gossamer glow of clarity, reflection, and subtlety.
And if you lack a sense of prosperity
call upon the Ursa meteors
to shower you with unexpected blessings.
And as you dwell in your seed,
call upon your highest self
to imagine a more peaceful earth
where you and ALL your sunflower kin
are encouraged and assisted to reach to the highest potential.

May we all sink our roots deep into this great mother
and live, love, and laugh
even when it seems dark beyond holy.
For IT IS a sacred moment
in our inner and outer earth's being.
Blessed be the Winter Solstice.

Mithra Deis Natalis Sol Invicti

(The Day of the Birth of the Unconquered Sun)

Cold and bleak, iron belly night cleaves.
Effulgence bursts forth,
burgeoning brilliance.
Chaste white gown, free from spot and blemish,
marries all as divinity,
too bright for mere sons of gods.

Snow swathed angels,
plopped from once pregnant heavens,
lie heavily in slumber in great nesting boughs.
The cradling limbs of their hosts
bow deeply in atonement:
radiance illuminating their reawakening.

Tiny ghost dancers leap and twirl,
pirouette in graceful syncopation,
flow like flocks of sheep in migration,
dance like Baptists in jubilation,
alight on cheeks,
disappear like faeries.
Nearly imperceptible kisses of joy
leave only a cool grace of knowing.

Breath's snowy owl wings
lift in crystallized exultation,
a rush of aliveness prickles
in awe-inspirited revelry.
The silent glistening rises like a humble prayer
in the bedazzling cathedral of promise.

In this in-between world,
eternity caught stillpoint,
brilliance floats between inhalation and exhalation.

No thing really exists here.
Strain to hear one voice
miss the host whispering from all that sparkles.

A pearl ring of iridescent bliss
encircles my kindling heart,
shimmers to greet the twinkling salvation.
All thought vaporizes
into the lustrous nacre of hallowed being.
And all that I am
dissolves into all that is.

Note: *Birth date attributed to both the ancient Persian and the Roman god, Mithra(s) associated with light and its salvation and the changing seasons. Birthday was celebrated Dec 25 predating Christianity.

Solstice Devotion

When the ground grew hard,
and the rivers froze,
grandma and grandpa knew
their time to rest was very close—
the harvest past, the animals safe,
the wood pile full to chock.
Her mead was honey yellow, his ale amber joy.
Their provisions all were stocked.

Grandpa would fetch in the Yule log
cleaved from the Maypole's spring blessing.
Grandma traced her fingers
along the ridges and rings, caressing.
She felt the wind that shook the branches
and the sun that fed it food—
knew the moisture in its heart,
could smell its earth-woven roots.

When the fall leaves were gone and animals hid,
when fragile life in frigid winds clung
grandma's scarves of soft blue spruce
on chimney shoulders hung,
and candles glowed from each great window
tucked in among the green array,
shimmering welcome to all returning
home to the shortest day,

grandpa would go out to check on the neighbors:
brought extra wood and a beacon of holiday cheer.
The bells on the horse's sleigh, jingling,
drove away all things to fear.
Then he would put out a plate from their meal
and a glass of his cider and a full corncob pipe
for the souls that wandered the land in need
on the longest and coldest of nights.

When the earth lay bare and wasted,
when all seemed lost in the black infested light,
grandpa lit the hearth fire blazing,
roasting chestnuts, waft delight.
then he mounded holly everywhere,
giving woodland spirits a warm and safe space.
Brightening berries called forth
joy from the dance of the harvest grace.

Tiny candles danced around the proud pine top
to help hold promise from the gloom.
Grandma festooned tiny sweet bundles
and hand-carved sacred runes.
She hung tiny bags of shiny coins,
and tempting trinkets galore,
to entice the secret tree spirits
to return in the spring once more.

When the shadows loomed, and we most despaired,
grandpa spread mistletoe high on every bow.
We sang, "Deck the Halls" and "Here Comes the Sun,"
to the whole world now.
Then they feasted us from their holy stores
to remind us all to trust.
We danced around and sang
and blessed the times that brought us thus.

Grandma fed us Clementines and ginger snaps
to remind us of the sun,
our salvation, our regeneration,
our unconquered one.
She sang, "Sun, sun, sun, here it comes."
We echoed, "Sun, sun, sun, here it comes."

Inevitable Processions

As he held witness
to the inevitable procession of great-souled beings,
a cavalcade of colossal, equine-vapor-spirit-bodies
drove across the swirled milky-tear and bruised bone colored sky.
The magnificent herd of cumulonimbus horse beings
coursed in orderly formation
with a great heaving, ribbed array of migration
that took up all his sight and mind.
The rumble of invisible hooves thundered hard
as they swept across the vastness of his desolate plain
and echoed in every canyon
that walled in his frozen, grief-streaked heart.
But their dark waters-of-life, ponderous underbellies
seemed to hold a precious promising.

Suddenly three great, thick-necked sky mustangs
emerged from their hidden wildernesses.
Two nearly fully-embodied galloping steeds
championed the whole sky to the north
while one became the west.
All their long, swooping, blue-grey muzzles
stretched down toward him
with swept-back ears and wind-flung manes.
He watched their sinuous cloud muscles pulse
in their etheric fibers,
and he thought he could almost feel
the wind spray from flaring nostrils.
Like water to water,
his own inner squalling suddenly bulged upward.
His eyes sought to atone with the heaven's bellies ripe to bursting,
and he surrendered to the life's burgeoning
that often requires death's midwifery,
tears from his eyes meeting, with grace, the skies
on the windowpane of his heart.

For Donald Sharp

She felt tipsy-canoodled, least that's what she said,
all muddy and puddly, her unjusts and her dreads
bewitched and befuddled, no ground in her head.
She simply lay down. She wouldn't be led.

A minute, a moment, sometime just to sink
deep down into the quench of a quiet soul's drink
from the eternal pool that sits far from the brink
of all the Huckabee's and Cruz's and other apocalyptic stink.

Her mind's tall grass a treasure, a sensory pleasure,
a nest she plopped into "beyond any measure."
Her daddy, the general, said, "Retreat ain't no bad gesture.
Rebuild your reserves for the next moment that tests ya."

Deep into a trance the walls became wrinkly.
Down through some wormhole she blinked twice to see
a Barack-headed rooster peck a Trump haired-twinkie.
Then he chased him into black nothingness with glee.

The dark, now around, was peaceful, calm, serene.
She felt pulled toward a light beyond an unseen stream.
She drifted on silence to follow a boat's dream,
emerged in her heart's grotto, a lush, tropical scene.

Thriving vines glistened, and great fruits festooned.
Showy flowers kissed her and bumbly bees crooned.
Thrumming hummingbirds whispered, "Let's fly to the moon."
All seemed welcome from the weave of light's loom.

She peered down into her pool, saw her radiance shine.
Took a sip from the water that's both yours and mine.
Surfed the ripple of connection beyond space and time
absorbed into the womb of consciousness sublime.

She didn't know how long she stayed there to heal,
swimming with dolphins and drifting with teals.
Her body grew stronger from her spirit's soul meals.
Glad memories erupted and called life to reveal.

She emerged from retreat full of strength and tenacity.
She felt rested, replenished, and full of vivacity.
Ready to rumble against the mean egos of audacity
of those who would question her spirit's veracity.

Note: From a time when Donald Sharp was ill.

Coal Chiseling Diamonds

In honor of Donald Sharp

His alabaster facade barely showed erosion
from the carving winds and etching floods of his many cycles.
Still, a slight sandstone shifting belied his timelessness.
His life had been full of the avalanches and earthquakes
that most spirit beings, walking in mineral vessels, had endured,
but he had seemed to rise above
the petty rubble-mind that plagued most.
Promising skies almost always seemed reflected,
glistening off the cornflower blue of his gem polished eyes.

He rose up from coal
to build a life of granite.
He was a stepping-stone, offering to others
a solid place to reach up from
with surety and accommodation.
His was not of the nature of scree,
not of the character
to let someone slip and trip and tumble down,
nor was he a slick-rock trickster,
nor rolling stone rambler.

His quartz propensities offered a sharp, multifaceted magnifier
with a conductive, yet prismatic wonder,
which forged him to be a focused hard worker and wise teacher.
His fluorite fluidity merged with his strength of iron,
and an insightful tiger's eye depth,
and a fine handed sculpting prevailed.
His turquoise and amethyst colorings
showed through in his fair-eyed trading
of the delicate stone children of others.
He was a spirit-being highly adept at shaping earthly tributes
and a poetic carver of self and stones.

And when the heat in his fire-opal passion rose up
and turned to the world's injustices and inhumanity,
his sharp chiseling tongue would nick
at the false veins of the Trumps and the McConnells,
and other boulders-blocking-the-river Republicans.
Or when admonishing President Obama
about the pyrite hypocrisies of sacrificing genius for the pragmatic
or railing from his granite pinnacles and high arches
about the absurdity and futility of war,
especially when the people's underpinnings were collapsing
and the world's weathers shifting to cataclysmic,
his was the hardpan wisdom of time immemorial.

In one of his final moments of presence on this plane,
he told Feather, "I'm just a bag of stones,"
then drifted off.

You may have ended as a bag of stones, my friend,
but many of them were diamonds!

Grace

He lived tormented
by what he saw frightened young men do
in the jungles of Vietnam,
especially to women and children.

His eyes bulged downward
into some abyss of captured soul wanderings.
Something clenched around his body,
as if a giant python
twisted and torqued his torso.
It trapped his breath until he clenched his fists.
He cranked his head sideways and upward
until his eyes puffed to tears
and peered directly into mine.

"And by what I had to do to women and to children
because of orders,"
he slowly added,
"and because I was afraid."

Wounded eyes, bulging wide, pleaded
through a bloody delta.
They searched mine briefly,
but could not accept grace.
His head bowed into his chest,
a python trying to devour a volcano.

Without looking up he continued,
"You never knew
if that smiling little boy
waving at you from the side of the path
might suddenly blow up,
killing your buddies.
Or if some pretty village woman

or an old grandmother
might come at you,
ready to kill you, even with just a knife.

"You had to respond.
You had to respond!"
he said almost feverishly,
then breathed deeply to gather some composure.
"It was hard to trust anyone,"
He trailed off to the silence that sliced our throats
and bled out our voices.

Alcohol had numbed him—
now was killing him.
Sleepless nights of horror, revisited
in countless dreams, no longer smothered down,
plagued him.

"I can't talk to anyone about this.
Can't burden my family.
Especially can't talk to the church."
He watched it kill his three older brothers.
They had all served together.
He asked if there might be a medicine man
who might offer a path more fitting for him
to find peace and understanding.
I told him I would get back to him.
I could only witness
with feelings of loving concern and ineptitude.
I sent him a name.

For a couple of years,
each time his body looking more gaunt,
his humor and presence eaten away,
I saw him,
he wouldn't respond to my inquiries anymore.

The thing that ate at him for 40+ years,

finally consumed him a few years ago.
That night when I heard of his journey,
I sent a drumming of easy passage.
I saw him rising through violet and magenta clouds,
boy-man face softly blue-lit, smiling.
His eyes beamed of reprieve.

An ecstatic enthusiasm raptured him.
He winged upward toward golden, shimmering light.
I saw him smile as if for the first time ever.
It eased the burden my heart carried.
A new day dawned
on the river of life.

The Art of Human Being

There is an art, of course,
from skilled potters, pens, and voices.
Some say art is only
two dimensioned oil choices.
But what about those who farm?
Or bake? Or usher in new inventions,
creating form and beauty and hallowed sight
beyond nature's known conventions?

There is an art that whispers up horses,
calms the skittish, balms the sick.
It can talk old chickens into laying
and shmooze donkeys not to kick:
fence and feed, herd and heed,
love and nurturance the mission.
Fathers showed how to work 'em,
but mamas taught how to listen.

There is an art that twirls up soufflés
that rival Rivieran breezes.
It coaxes delicate profiteroles
to guilt-be-damned capricious.
It bests Napoleons and Wellingtons
with measured strength and subtle croons.
It builds replicas of the "Pieta"
out of orange biscotti and macaroons.

There is an art that summons up Macgiver spirit
to mend with paper clips and old sinew.
It makes a hearty neighborhood feast
from autumn's last elk slew.
It can dance with chainsaws, Harleys, backhoes
that all purr to the touch,
while sporting silk panties under long johns,

beauty and function both a must.

There is an art that gathers the trashy cast-away
to sculpt rusty garden resurrections.
It wildcrafts sacred spirit flowerings
to better health, love, and protection.
It dances to the silent beat
of stars and wind and fireflies.
It inflames the souls of witnesses
just by shining in their eyes.

It doesn't really matter
if you're trained, self-taught, or avatar.
Art, it seems, will show up
when your flow is from your heart.
It doesn't really matter what you choose
to work or play or do.
Art is just what happens
when you let life work with you.

To The Table

His scatter-shot mind
blasts everything with a weak-scoped, tunneled visioning.
Bullets squeal wind empty.
They knick unbridled notions, graze grizzle-boned gnawings,
trying to just take one down with some meat on it,
gut it,
skin it,
filet its prime cuts,
marinate it in enticing spices,
fuse it with comforting and exotic compliments,
serve it flambe' entrancing tableside.

Oh, to offer it up to the gush of the fine poetry dining patrons
come together in communion
for their once weekly breaking fast
from everyday trump steak and potato banalities.

But his hunting light swiftly grows dark,
and too much of his game seems old and tough to chew,
and there is not enough energy to pound it to a tender morsel,
nor time enough to coax it to a sophisticated ambrosia of a stew.

And he curses that so much is hash rehashed,
the same old offerings fried in new grease
with the same old onions and peppers,
just the same-old long exposed to air-rottings,
trying to be chef's choice.

He wants gastronomic utterances
and a grace of taste and texture
to gift a word gourmand's tongue and ears.
He craves a slaking from jabbering grub and vacuous victuals.
But all he can cook up is a chintzy chop suey.

No Poem Today

He mused among his many meanderings,
traipsing mercilessly to and fro
between crumbling mountain majesties
and molehill Magdalena maudlinacies.
But his mangy mind mongrels mostly masticated
all his mis-shaped mobilizations with enmity.
No poem today.

He palavered a parliament
of petulant peevishnesses.
They perforated his purposeful ponderances
with suppressed pissant improprieties,
which posited prickles surreptitiously.
No poem today.

He ruminated ravenously,
raking rambunctious reminiscences
around ragtag relativities.
He realized rascally recollections
too ribald for recounting
and rarely wrangled roustings
that rendered raw recoilings.
No poem today.

He dreamed, and he drummed, and he deliberated.
He drifted defunct and direly debilitated.
He even demanded his deities deliver
delicious descriptive dollops
that demonstrated drooling *de riguer*.
No poem today.

He felt all fracked, cracked, and patty wacked,
His didactic pacts
seemed all trite and hacked.

So he jacked the act and bivouacked,
the sacking was a time worn fact.
Such is his poem today.

Some Man's Garden

Bright mornings found him intoning
sacred songs of Mel and Bing.
Soul stirred daisies and petunias
massed to hear him sing.
He had chants for the chrysanthemums,
many *om mani padme oms*,
but crooned Frank to the Lady Slippers,
swore they trembled near to swoon.

Judy, Babs, and Liza belted out
to hollyhocks stoic and unimpressed,
and the Nasturtiums liked the 50's,
but anything Elvis was best.
The primrose only wanted songs
that were really really sad,
while the honeysuckle kept moaning
they needed Harry Connick "real bad."

Like Kelly splashed in puddles,
he rain danced and sang of bliss,
shook the dryness off his lily,
gave his organza a wet kiss.
"The Sun"ll Come Out Tomorrow"
burst out on endless rainy days.
Thunder defiant falsetto vibrato
seemed to sweep away all haze.

And when the full moon rose up
you'd find him flitting to and fro,
acting out the whole performance
of the Rocky Horror Picture Show.
"Time Warping" with datura,

"Building a Man" for San Pedro,
"I'm Going Home" for all the buddies
that wound up having to let go.

But the roses just wanted Broadway,
Cabaret, Carousel, Camelot.
And they would sway with ribald adoration
at any campiness they got.
Especially when his inner diva belted out
"Everything's Coming Up Roses,"
the cocky posies vogued
their pretty petulant poses.

And he sang exuberant songs
to the prickly pear and wild peonies,
tunes of intuitive gibberish
amid loud cacophony,
because he knew their thinking
that most of the songs were fine,
but that they had just been flattened out
by too many Hammers and Steins.

Full Athena

She took off the crown of her head
down by a slow trickling riverside
and emptied it into the moon-faced pond
at one end of her yesterdays.
Boxes of rain were delivered to her,
and she tenderly caressed
her incensed strongholds with them.
The nine swords of saints and fools
begged within her grasp.
Her bare of root rise
up pride slicing rungs of karmic razors
broke raw, vain winds to exhaust.
Fevered tendrils that still thrashed
from her frenzied hacking out of Zeus's head
let succumb their grasp.
The night owl sat on her throne now.
She cooed as her sub-fused sirens
sluiced into her soul, thirsting arroyos
emptying her
into her calm blue eternal pool.
Breathing in the cadence
of the cicadas in the sashaying willows,
she drank the orderly milk of the stars.
She rested,
trusting.

Magdalena de Luz

Her ablution,
rolling in the first morning's dew,
whispered before petals
yawned to stretch—

her oblation,
consecrated licking of creek ferns clean
from the cloaking of their darkness—

her binding,
the piercing thrum of the earth
to brilliant omnipotent silence,
golden star's shaft
humming her root—

her bonding,
caressing giddy like a thousand pansies,
the musky body of her eternal lover,
inner jubilation frolics—

her benediction,
tumbling amongst the immodest sky archings
of stiff sunflower minarets,
swaying their bawdy beseechings—

her balm,
Melissa shimmying in her skimpy virga
to juniper whisperings of long forgotten love songs—

her obligation,
to bear witness to the patch of prickly pear
enthralled like first posting.
She sits, delicate cactus flower, pregnant like patience—

her beneficence,
a spiraling vortex of honey bees
enveloping her in a shimmering shroud,
gathering blossoms
to deliver the fragrance of purity's bliss
to the world believing suffering—

her benevolence, raptured: she is reborn,
her nakedness without sin,
her openness without shame,
bee queen of the universe.

Secret Ingredients

Unapologetic as champagne,
one knew where she brewed,
haughty *foie gras* heart,
disdainful of stew.

Day dreamy like mac and cheese,
mild cheddar colored mood,
soft whipped up potatoes,
his Terpsichorean 'tude.

From his buff hot house tomato
to her impeccable asparagus,
like bitter greens and balsamic,
they always tossed a tantalizing test

of how two people so different
could ever make a match
when one is Beluga caviar
and the other corned beef hash.

He's friendly like pot pie.
All types of veggies and chicken get along well,
always with a leg up or a breast to cry on
if someone felt like hell.

At first date she held Wellingtons at six
ransomed Napoleons at eight,
dashed brandy drawn battle lines
if he dared ever be late.

But some secret sauce emerged
in the pairing of the two
and over time a mellowing
like ripple and *port du salut*.

His buttermilk took out her game
whatever it did take.
And now they share communally
like chocolate raspberry decadence cake.

Polar Shifts

Flourishing raven wings
briskly wick aloft
to vanish in cosmic slight of hand.
They laugh like karmic fools to pretentious kings.
Shimmering ripples
lap the shores of closed-eye lands,
all lonely desperadoes tucked beneath shields
girded safe against the blue-petaled inquisition,
and the sun's unrelenting quest for truth.
What matters
when we either fly too close to the sun,
ashing to star dust,
or veer away
as dead potatoes into cold deep space?
Will we just be humans
fracking up some other Eden elsewhere?

If It Takes A Village

In his small village
everyone knew everyone.
If a man fell down
cursing his fate,
questioning his lot
in the middle of the road,
everyone would listen.
Drunk or sober,
in tongues or in tears,
they knew he was talking to God.
In his small village the people,
their hearts, would be open
for the wound
and for the wonder.

In his small village,
watching with leopard eyes,
there and not,
the people would sweep their porches
and reflect their paths.
The people would share their beans
and breathe their humanity.
The people would feed their verdant plants
as well as their dry, barren-soul patches
with the community waters.
For it was for all to use.
Such was their sacred trust of rain,
and of grief.

In his small village
the people would hold sacred witness
for that man or that woman or that child
who poured out onto the earth.
They would keen pleas at God's feet

for mercy, or sanity, or forgiveness, or love.
Patiently they entranced
until the god talker was spent,
wrenched empty,
surrendered like a lump of lifeless clay.

Then the people would pick that person up,
carry them to the river,
bathe them with silky yucca root,
gentle them with calming herbs and oils and caresses,
swathe them in rabbit pelt swaddling,
and place them in their clean bed.
All the while a feast was prepared to honor the sacred communion.

In his small village
the people were the balm of God.
The people shared their tears, like manna from heaven,
so that each and every one was fed and comforted.

"My small village is no more," he cried.
I heard his forlorn tale of how his small village
was smothered by a landslide while he was away:
how everyone was gone,
that he was the last one left,
felt how, now alone, he felt he needed to water his own trust.
I saw him weep in the cold sterile box of television.
I felt myself terribly saddened, wondering,
"Is there even a village left
that would bathe and swaddle any of us?
How could we forget?"

Earth Day

An American Indian man paddled
into the consciousness of America.
Skimming his canoe through water no longer clear
as it was in his grandfather's time.
His broad shoulders worked against the river's current,
no longer pristine, but oily in swirls and syrupy in clumps
of greedy neon greens and smothering oranges and jaundiced yellows.
A dead fish floated along beside.
A dross of broken bottles, empty cans, used paper goods,
and disposable plastics bloated the waters all about him.
The castaways of factories, farms, and everyday humans
swept down to him, strangling the green banks surrounding him.
The dead soul entrails of the ignorant ethos
of a self-centered, consuming society
littered the waters and shoreline and land as far as he could see.
He paddled against 150 years of industrial waste deemed "success."
He paddled against the mindset of get more, faster,
and easier than before, regardless of the cost.
He paddled against 400 years of lands stolen,
scourged, and disrespected,
and of peoples and creatures decimated
in the name of Manifest Destiny and "progress."
His one tear running down his face,
as he surveyed what once was everyone's water of life,
once sparked the world to action.
Do you remember?

Evolution

The eagle pair, circling the outcropping,
proclaimed to him,
"You are eternal spirit being
sailing in an ephemeral ship of state.
Ride the wave!"

The worms in his spring garden bed
chanted at him,
"Be aware of all empty passionless voyages
without destination or cause."
 The rabbit squirming in a rising hawk's talons
screamed at him,
"You may be susceptible to rogues and pirates.
Guard your booty well and wisely.
But when it's gone, you must let it go."

The chipmunks nesting inside his engine
asked him,
"Would you really chuck it all for a "fairytale oasis?"

The rust on his wheezing tractor
whispered to him,
"You're just gonna' work 'til the day you die!"

His dog just grinned at him,
his tail aquiver like a boat's propeller
and affirmed through adoring eyes,
"I love you forever."

Will I Find You in the Wilderness?

She implored,
"Oh my beloved,
where have you gone?
I bubble in cauldrons of love and fire,
trying to understand meaning amidst bombs and beauty,
hoping to discern bullets of pain, ambiguous from projection,
wanting to hear kindness from clutter."

She pleaded,
"I struggle to understand.
Swirling vapors of meanings fog about my head.
I am challenged to not presume psychic shrapnel
from impressions below emissions.
My hope fears being abandoned
by possible enlightenments floating off into oblivion.
I am afraid I seem callous or apathetic—
for I often know not what to say in response,
in compassion.
Then I become the missing.
Why do you desert me?
Why do I desert me?"
She bent, beaten by her own lash.

She questioned, "Did I call you?
Are you the wall to hide me from all my ballistic fathers?
Are you the screen to save me
from all my nattering, chattering mothers?
Are you the wilderness I have always wanted to escape to?
Yet, when I seek humbled silence amidst nature's beckoning nirvana,
I am distracted by Your insistence on being heard.
Amid chirping birds and bright blue skies you yak at me,
and sadness threatens to consume me.
Among the hum of thriving flora and fauna
you buzz in my head alone.

Are you now the evil tyrant?

She mused,
"It is said something is not taken
without something else becoming stronger in its place to compensate.
The healer told me that I could hear things
that other people couldn't imagine.
Is that what you bring for me?
A psychic knowing?
You leave me to just trust my gut.
You leave me to just trust.
You leave me.
But am I abandoned?"

Note: *this is about my relationship to my hearing difficulties; a punctured eardrum, tintinitus, small ear canals. It is addressed to my hearing, the clarity of my hearing, and my hearing as a question of purpose to "God".

Punks

Finally inside,
away from their prying eyes,
feeling mugged,
fatigued from the constant siege
by crazy young gods out on a rampage
he is unsettled.

He steels, cold-boned,
and freezes doe-eyed,
behind too thin windows.
He is edgy,
like mice with long-armed cats roaming about.

They were here just days ago, he thinks.
They always seem to come
in the changing times.
He could barely forget
their kicking sand in his face,
toppling his sandcastles.

Just over the brink
the feisty ruffians, barely at bay,
hurl spiky shards of crackly, frigid breath about.
Their brutal, icy fingers pinch at noses
and tweak ears.
Their fierce fists punch
with stinging and blinding curses.
They howl with abandon,
and he shudders.
Ancient survival fears rouse
among savage greetings and warnings.
Tormented mockeries worm-hole into consciousness
through the psychic eggshell cracklings
of wind chimes, porch chairs, buckets, and boards

clanged together,
ripped apart,
and tossed haphazard in a riot without mercy.

He must go out again.
He dreads it.
He senses them
ganging down driveways, running amok,
startling.
He fears their whipping around corners,
hurtling over fences,
nosing into hidey holes.
They blow up in everyone's faces,
beat on hunched over shoulders,
and bay at the heels of the edgy sheep.
They fray flags and nerves alike,
the Zuni "Mad Winds of March," punks on a rampage.

BOOK II

POETIC PORTRAITS

Neptune's Lover

I climbed the last barrier dune,
the biggest one.
Sultry ocean scent pulsed up against my ecstatic ethers.
I tasted the tang of air on my lip-moistening tongue.
The billowing breath caressed my flesh
like a rough handed, but gentle lover.
Its balm stung in my nostrils
and surged a wave in my being.
It splashed me awake,
yet seduced me to dreams
in the same soft, yet dangerous whisper
made only by the sea.

I had always thought the sea was a man
since the day I awoke to my voice having fallen
and then later, that same day, nearly drowning.
On that day a handsome man dove to save me.
I was too far out and being carried further away by the current.
He swam like a mystical sea creature.
He wrapped a strong, muscular arm around my chest,
around my grateful heart,
and cradled me to him as he lifted me to salvation.
Our hearts seemed to beat as one
in synch with the ocean's sweeping metronome.
The smell of the sea merged with my hero's caring
and my own swamping adoration.
It smacked my senses into an alchemical stupor
that to this day can muddle me up.
I knew it then, and it felt like a tsunami of divine mystery.
I hand tattooed a tiny merman
on my left hand's ring finger to affirm it.
That day, at 12,
I secretly married the King of the Sea.

I pushed up the steepness
against the sand, against time taking back
old blood steaming in my veins,
young breath dreaming in my mind.
A stiff wind headed my sails.
I knew he called for me.
I heard his celestial sea voice singing,

"Come to me,
please come to me.
Oh, how happy we will be
in our kingdom of the sea!"

And as I had done so many times before
I rushed, a wave propelled
back to the engulfing love of my eternal mate.

Suddenly I remembered Hawaii,
the stories of those swept away
when they turned their backs to the sea,
and I vowed an open-hearted reunion
through time eternally.

I mounted the dune's great rise
and stood solid against my great love's rush.
I held sway against his lips that brushed.
His cool breath licked at me
and lapped away my beads of sweat.
He welcomed me home like a good lover longed for.
His lip-parted smile inhaled me into him.
A timeless bliss enveloped me.
I knew he came to devour me,
and in his roaring silence
I let him.

Suddenly,
I startled at a popping sound
down on the beach,

muffled, but distinct.
I cocked my head toward no one and nothing
except golden sand and sea drift treasures.
In my soft, focused gaze I saw it coming:
something there, yet not,
round and spinning.
It winged through the morning sea haze
of another time and space.
I saw it a few feet in front of my eyes,
spiraling right toward me,
and I knew, without feeling any pain,
that a ball slug bore into my forehead
and pierced my skull and brain.
It ripped apart reality and left a dime sized hole,
but yet, not.
Everything seemed quiet and oddly plain.

In that instant,
the knowing that I had once been killed there
merged with the fact that I lived there now,
whole and standing.
I stood alone on the dune overlooking the pristine bay,
understanding that a bullet
had just let a timeless wind into my skull.
The cool sea breeze licked into the psychic wound
with caring concern
while the sea god's immortal tongue
flickered into my soul's yearning.
I closed my eyes into surrendered bliss.

The split seam of time rippled close
against consciousness.
I witnessed chaos and confusion.
I glimpsed the bay from long ago
and spied the sleek tri-masted ship at anchor
and suddenly knew myself as a pirate.
Then I saw a shipmate fire
and also knew myself as thief,

and all the while I knew myself
as the eternal lover
of the man of the sea.
And I knew
that once a seaman, always a seaman,
and that the waters would always wash me free.

Illegitimi Non Carborundum!

(Don't Let the Bastards Grind You Down)

Toppled chariots
from old crashing nightmares
left rusting in the dreary tearing of his mind,
embedded
in the lethargy of his wheeling limbs,
but still he stands impudent against death's capture.

A long, long time ago
he had come back from the war.
Shot down behind enemy lines, prisoner for two years,
he returned from being starved and beaten and tortured,
came back to his new wife and child after being kept in a box
for his sassy lip and his many attempts to escape.
He had lost half his weight
and most of his peace—
before becoming
a liberated prisoner for a lifetime.

For a while it was good:
horse racing,
his children growing,
his wife happy.
Then a nail shot out from under his lawn mower
pierced death into his eldest son's heart,
sent his own heart back into the torturing box.

A sneering facade erupted.
He found a multitude of men to beat.
He found a multitude of peoples to hate.
He found an angry, wrathful, Old Testament God inside himself,
and he looked out through steely eyes,

dragged down, weighted by ancient chains magnetized
by the cold iron of his blaming and resentful heart.

The slight, raised snarl of his left lip
always meant danger.

He cursed his children.
Cursed his life
Cursed his fate.
Only his wife stood by him
until she succumbed to a cancer eating her.
He called her a saint and then cursed his darkness.

He creaked forward,
an ancient man with a prehistoric mind,
lost in his own world, impervious,
his soul trapped back in another time.
Unforgiving,
leaving little but a beaten old jalopy
to weather in achingly slow demise,
the clutching skeletons in the stifling old folk's home,
the last guards of his capture,
felt hassled at his ever-menacing lip,
a dinosaur not ready to die.

Numbered Days

(1)

She began to count them
on her 3,650th morning of being alive.
It was the day the class sang a song of celebration of her.

The next morning a metallic red heart decal appeared
on the giant wall calendar of cuddly kittens
in the box of November 24
with its neon pink high-lighted #3650
in large characters,
calling to witness.

And every day from then on,
a number appeared on each consecutive day
on the calendar of her wall:
#3651,
#3652,
#3653,
each with hearts following.
For those were good days then.

And she looked back on her life
and noted in her diary,
"On morning #1 I cried, I guess.
On my 297th morning I took my first steps,
my baby book says.
On my 2197th morning
I entered the first grade and threw up."
A hand drawn little, frowny face appeared beside the entry.
"On #3022, Baby Johnny came."
She placed double hearts there.
On her 3650th day, she noted, "They love me,"
and a long line of hearts trickled off the page.

(2)

Many hearts,
and a few frowns,
spread across the many flips of time.
As the young girl grew,
as she counted her days in gratitude,
she rejoiced in her life.

On the morning of #4876,
her Uncle Jimmy came up behind her in the laundry room,
reached around from behind and squeezed her breasts.
She shot out from his arms and against the wall,
cowering with wide, disbelieving eyes.

"Don't you dare tell, you little slut.
No one will believe you!"
He snarled down at her,
shoving a finger toward her face.
That night
she couldn't bring herself to even look at the calendar.
Grief and angst clutched her awake
with only a few soul-scorched snatches of dreamtime.

The next day
her Uncle Jimmy raped her,
forced her down in the laundry room,
said he'd kill her if she told.

The numbers stopped
as understanding stopped,
as joy stopped,
as hunger stopped,
as the will to live stopped.
She became a drowning woman in endless time.
A black eddy of despair sucked the will out of her.
Nothing and no one could get her to eat,
or talk,

or play.
She went to school and hid
behind her cold, dead eyes,
looking up from the bottom of her black swamp.

But Uncle Jimmy kept on.
He dogged her,
sniffed at her and licked his lips,
rubbed at himself with menacing leers,
yanked her clothes and arms,
almost bruising her.

But he made her
begin to count again.

She hatched a plan.
She counted the days till she might be free,
and she counted each day with a new determination.
Four mornings later,
she set up her father's recorder
above the drying stacks
before Uncle Jimmy threatened his return.
She wasn't sure she would survive it.
She knew she was no longer willing to feel dead from it,
and she captured Uncle Jimmy
with his cruel, selfish yearnings and sent him to prison,
#1942 emblazoned over his heart.

(3)

She never did count her days again.
A new normal was mostly a mix of hard and worse days.
She watched them roll through
from her many dungeons and balconies.
After many years
she found a kind and patient woman
in the support group she went to.
She trembled and screamed many nights into her arms

and learned a way to love and trust again.
She learned that she was not evil.
She finally forgave Uncle Jimmy, who was murdered in prison.

She adopted 2 kids
and lived a long, long time.

The Box

She remembered back
to when she had finally begun to pull the strips apart.
She felt the screaming tweezings of fate's coarse weavings
from twisted skeins, which once entangled
her morals and wishes and unyielding "needs"
into a tapestry hung of repugnant humors
and sweltering contempt—
all shame deadened on public gallows
and buried in the coffin about her heart.

Today she marked time with a candle
to the memory of her liberator.
She could still feel his soft, caring cheek
caressed against her teary one,
could hear his sweet, hot breath
whisper piercingly into her ear.

"I hear you! I love you!
Come play on the hills with me."
His soul-filled eyes
melted the ice that daggered her heart.
They begged a frolic that would kick-start her spirit's greatness
and gallop with her across barren wastelands
and carry her to the eternal springing pool
for a long, cool quench
that would slake her confusion and distrust
and lead to the understanding
that no box could ever contain.

She had learned to value the box over time.
She found satisfaction in it as retreat,
as rebuilder,
as safe haven and hermitage,
and as portal to other dimensions.

The teachers had come when she was ready.
They had held and loved and befriended
the cursing, exiled demons of ugly demandings
sent there by a child adrift in an ocean of loneliness.
They helped her to realize the emptiness, vast
like her mother's oblivious gossip streamings,
and suffocations
like her Uncle Billie's oily touch on her waters.

The strips of the tapestry's
once blood-enraged red cords
now turned to forgiving pinks.
The threatening sky's black and blues
burst forth with silver lines of trust,
with surrender threading amongst them.
And the murky yellows of past regrets
and shames and fears
now hung as golden silks of compassion.

Her once rigid thatchings became
softened to supple unfoldment
by the torrents of grief that had deluged upon them
after the lightning struck,
and her tower fell
when her rains had spilled upon her scorched, rutted earth.
Then the big-eyed deer had come
to lick her soul clean as she lay splayed and vulnerable.
And the songbirds had come to sing her back to dignity.
Then she flew with wild abandon,
enveloped in the wild earth-trembling
upon the sweat drenched, heaving back
of her passion-stoked savior.

Many lives seemed to have passed in her yesterdays.
And through many roustings had she learned her dignity.
She had come to know the value of the box.
And now she kept her false teeth in one
on the bed-stand by her lamp.

The River And The Stone

Jimmy swept up people
like flotsam in his stream;
served customers at tables
to titters, hoots, and screams,
huggy-kissed all the women,
made men red and yellow and green.
They bobbed along quite helpless
'til gasping out, "Oh, queen."

John was a banker,
the rock in any storm.
He looked all souls in the eye,
made folks feel safe and warm.
Tellers praised him kindly.
Friends said, "Not the norm."
He anchored many people
in the coursing of their storms.

They met in Old Havana,
both fleeing from the cold.
Jimmy wanting something new;
John feeling somewhat old.
In a neighborhood bodega
the same plantain they grabbed to hold.
John's big eyes met Jimmy's
and something shimmered besides his gold.

Jimmy sashayed close to John,
fruit still in each one's hand,
kissed him squarely on the cheek,
said, "Ooh, lover man.
I'm usually not this forward,
but you sure could change my plans
'cause my hand is round your plantain,

and my heart's in cha cha land."

John the rock rolled with abandon,
splashed the stream of Jimmy's delight.
Cuba *libra* welled his senses,
spelled the fierceness of his night.
They marengued through the alleys,
hiding kisses 'neath soft light,
gathered honeysuckle smoldered caresses
under the moon's magnolia white.

On a pearl's back beach they made love,
far from all prying eyes—
though Jimmy could have done it
with anyone standing by.
John would keep his reputation;
his decorum made him shy.
A rock he was, a rock he'd be
until the day he died.

Jimmy's waters swamped his banks.
Teary-thanks, like fishes, teemed.
John's heart soared to think of Jimmy
forever washing his rock-heart clean.
Somewhere before the dawn
cracked open its soul-filled seams,
they strolled to John's cabana
and fell asleep to cuddling dreams.

Tree Rings

She remembered her spindly growth when young,
remembered the old resentments toward those that seeded her;
how she had thought their pious fear of drought
had kept her small and weak,
offered her little but some old family dirt,
just enough water to want more,
and an oppressive shade that forbade
a brazen standing in glory.
She had wanted so much more back then:
just to shake off her branches
and loose them from their confined coursings
in the full love of her solar granddaddy.

She remembered her very first big leaving,
swept away silently in the night,
carried off by some tall oak's limbs.
She had found herself lost,
stuck in Needles with two sprouts
and an ever-drifting partner's shadow.
The thought of the saving Greyhound
as she whisked her kids away still rocked her.
The lurching mix of toilet cinnamon,
old bitter Micky D's coffee,
and the drunk pee-smelling man passed out on the last seats
could still smack her senses around.
But they were three seeds
stuck on the hoof of the karmic-cow heading east
as she thirsted in the sun once more,
the joy in her soul still timeless.

From that moment on
she followed to where her leaves blew.
She roamed the lands with her two treelings,
ever-widening their vistas and freshening their views.

She found herself flowering in the nurturing of many others.
She nestled many fallen birdlings in the bowers of her being.
She rejoiced in having coaxed once shy songbirds
to belt out showtunes.
Over time, abused and beaten down young starlings,
by the scores, had escaped to her sanctuary
and remembered how to share in love once more.
One day she even returned to her old grounds,
brought some fertilizers of forgiveness and humility
and planted new shoots to someday blossom.
She hoped anyway.
But she believed she had re-sod the generations of barren soil.
And though many hard and cold seasons
had coarsened her bark, she could look back now
and know the rings of her tree would always bind her with love
and that her gnobby roots would always let her roam with trust.

Harbor Waves

All vain foundations will crumble;
trust faults will quake and crack.
Worry, all tyrants:
here comes the karmic wave smack.

Boundaries are destructive
where human plates converge.
The blood and tears you displace
will call humanity to surge.

The multitudes of tiny waves,
skimming across your seas,
one by one are "harmless,"
but be aware, O King Tyranny!

Those tiny waves will rouse
the people's greatest urge
to live free and be happy
and will roar up like a scourge.

Once suppressed yearning,
churning all the people's pleas,
will swell up defiant against
the trump of ill dignity.

You won't have a place to run
when the harbor waves climb—
when the tsunami wave of justice
comes to humble you for your crimes.

You'll watch your shoreline vanish
as your sky-mind begins to shatter,
and in a cosmic ass whoopin',
nothing else will matter.

It may not be tomorrow.
It still may take a while.
Many tortured, many killed,
hardly reasons to find a smile.

And it may not even be this life.
The next or next may hand
an age's old atonement
for a tower that cannot stand.

So, my trust line has not broken.
Your payment will come due,
and, in the end, blossoms will bloom
from the dirt that makes you, you.

In the Desert

The plaint softly arose.
It swept amid him and the tweeting small bird's
first light rambling in the sagebrush and mesquite trees.
It skirted his java edged shadow and light assimilations
where brazen beams swamped his Gollum-cave sensitivities.
He watched a lone coyote scamper along a dune slit facade
and then up and over a broken link out of sight.
He felt its eyes still watching him from the shadow.
He liked being in shadow too, he thought.

The elegy came again.
A subterranean tonal quaking
chipped away at the rock walls of his yawning chasmic
and looming colossus-strewn morning-mind.
He huddled at the edge of his small fire,
his morning meanderthal muttering complaints.
He began his usual exorcising
as his slick and slippery, scree-riddled dreamtime
tried bridging his clamoring day-dreadings.
Still, the blue-sparked cooing
touched his inside land like far off lightning.
Napalm brandishing red ants
soldiered along his ignorant placements,
marshaling to capture his sweetness,
and stung to fire his fortifications.
He leapt to jog a jolting jig,
incendiary searing calling to full battle station.
Amid the war cries and counter defenses,
he cursed his uncaring God, his cheating wife,
and his trumping partners
while the desert around succumbed to sentinel stillness.

Free at last, he bivouacked a few yards away,
burnings and yearnings still blistering under his skin.

And then he heard it,
the sad and forlorn "hoo, hooo" of some seeking creature
softly carried by the breeze.
And again it came, "hooo, hoooo,"
and his ears and heart pitched to its soul-trumpeting.
And once more it came,
and he heard it ask, "hooo …hoooo, will miss you? Hooo?"
Its hallowed lamentation welled in his throat,
consecrating his loneliness,
commiserating in his barrenness,
and he wept,
calling the desert to bloom once more.

Caw of the Wild

Cracking through
her maudlin mindings,
a raven's shrill gracking
hi-jacked into her eternal now.

She lifted her earthbound brow
from yesterday's strangling sorrows
that clutched her tomorrow's tears
to witness her gypsied joy.

She trailed two embossed, black jewel lovers' entwined bewitchings
that coursed against the blue petals of the sun's outward flowering.
Flashing wings briskly warped and wove,
vanishing and reappearing in cosmic prestidigitation.

Crafty magpie laughter, wicked
from among the swaying shaggy bark arms,
pregnant pinion bellies, and stratus piercing ponderosa torsos,
mocked all earthbound blasphemies.

She swept herself into
the mesmerizing, synchronal spiral looping
of the terpsichorean love emissaries.

She inhaled and exhaled their slow-tatting
of a new weave to ever-changing mystery.

And she felt clean.

Christmas Eve Mastications

The restaurant was packed.
The maître' d sat him right beside
the ever-whapping French door service entrance.
He stifled his resentment toward the injustice,
a snarl nipping at his upper left lip
like a catfish taking bait.
The *Zuppa Di Pesce* arrived,
a hair swimming with cod and mussels.
Tapping the table with impatience,
a butter pat somersaulted, splat,
onto his dry-cleaned sleekness.
He clenched his lips together
to hold the barracuda at bay,
wanting only fish of peace this night.

He recalled his wife this morning
telling him she was leaving for another "trip."
He had gasped on his bitter greens
while his bread sopped tears of implications.
He took stock in the *Scungilli Fra Diavollo*,
so many lifeless arms languishing limply,
like his so many dashed dreams
that wanted to live on the street named "Easy."
Slippery squid bellies caught him off guard,
made him remember when he and his little brother
tried to see who could keep a frog in their mouths longer.
Then they reminded him of his need to tell his boss
that his investments had lost the company a good client,
lots of money, and was leading to an audit.
He tried to remember who
the patron saint of Italian fishermen was,
thinking maybe a prayer could help.
But he couldn't remember anymore.
He could only see mama wagging a damning finger at him

in his face at Christmas long ago
for trading his little brother's new boots for a bag of pot.
He stared down at his cannoli feeling impotent.
He polished off the wine bottle.

"I'll get right with you tomorrow," he muttered,
dropping his eyes quickly from a small picture of Jesus
suddenly sadly staring at him
from behind the reception desk.
He crossed himself automatically.
He drove home, straight through three red lights,
and passed out on the sofa,
Wayne Newton singing Silent Night.

Prophesied

She had end times fear!
She believed Satan was gathering all his powers.
He was using all his methods to mislead the people.
He would keep them safe, he promised.
He would make them rich, he bragged.
He would make them proud of their old heritage
because they were better than those others,
the different ones,
the alien ones,
the untrustworthy users from shithole places ones.
She feared the hounds of hell secretly chewed at the bones
of liberty, decency, and even life,
gorging on the bloody excess
in the sulfuric bowels of a once great house.

She believed they herded the sheepish masses
toward a reckoning cliff,
their razor fangs shredding civilities.
Alpha bullies devoid of morals demanding obeisance,
raking liberties, flouting ethics,
placating their lusts with shameless satiations,
their bayings confusing, disorienting, mocking,
their beastly ends justified by any means.
She was sure, and she was scared.
The Antichrist was slick-tongue-tweeting,
making Armageddon great again.

Under the Gypsy Moon

The young village man came upon the old Gypsy's wagon,
smoke curling from his chimney,
as the mighty winds squealed and slapped.
Instead of running like he normally might,
he knocked because he was freezing.
The ancient spirit-eyed man looked him over quickly
and then invited him in.
As the young man sat
in the comforting, quiet place full of bright clothes,
candles, musky incense, and a vast array
of items from worlds unknown,
a hot mug of mulled wine warmed his hands and stomach.

He decided to ask the kind-faced man,
"How do you face the long night alone
when the sun seems lost and black fear reigns?"

The old Romani wistfully recalled for the youth,
"Under our gypsy sun,
when my family still lived,
we were the royalty of the roadway.
Our brightly colored caravan of wagons would come to your town,
appearing as if from thin air in the morning's dew laden field.
We came to share.
We brought our strong forgings of fine metal goods to hawk
and our earth-precious weavings.
We came to tinker pots and pans,
farm your fields, and pick your harvests.
My family bottomed your chairs,
caught your rats,
smithed your horses,
and mended your bellows.
And then we all would play our fine instruments
and sing and dance for you.

That was our most precious offering,
to lift your spirits and spread our peace and joy,
for we needed each other.
And if you crossed our palms with silver,
we would foretell whatever you wished to know
and some of what you'd rather not.
My mother was renowned for her gifts.
She could tell you
where your fortune lay and what must be done to claim it,
where sat your love and what magic to gain it,
what ailed your flesh and what we carried to cure it.

And when the fox was at your henhouse, or death outside your door,
sometimes she could even help you beat it before it got you, this
      time.

In return,
we Romani only asked for what we needed to follow the wind
and to live our truth.
And if you treated us poorly,
and cheated our work of its rightful dues,
we might bring some karmic release to you,
then disappear like phantoms in the night."
He winked a sly wink,
a sadness remembered in his face.

Then the old man suddenly beamed,
"But each night, under the gypsy moon
when our family would gather,
we claimed our kinship with the star beings.
Ever called to wander,
we rejoiced our way across the galaxy.
We played our strings of heaven
and sounded the mystic calls of the cosmos.
I can still hear how our violins wept unspoken tears
and the pipes compelled laughter
of the innocent child in us all.
With a rhythmic twist of skirt and tinkle of bell

and a lilt of foot,
we caught the spark of everyday soul
from our night's campfire
and lifted it to paradise.

It was our beloved duty to sing and dance
into the night in celebration of it's, and our, divinity.
The old man grew silent.
The youth looked at him quizzically,
"But you still haven't answered
how you face the bleak, hopeless night."

The old man just stared at the ground.
"My culture has been mocked, cursed at, lied about,
enslaved, and put in ghettos,
run out, and disbanded,
forced to assimilate or else.
Millions, like my own mother and father and uncles,
were murdered by Hitler's thugs,
let alone by all the other places that did not understand our ways
and tried to blame us or tame us or exterminate us."

The bent gypsy looked up to meet the young man's eyes,
"How do I face the bleak, hopeless night?

"As long as I can see an open highway on the earth
or in the heavens, I am strong.
As long as I can remember the rumble of the creaky wagons
or the clack of gay castanets,
or sing the song of the rustling trees, I am happy.
As long as I have friend wind at my back
and feel the enchanting pulse of the earth through my feet,
I will endure.
Under the gypsy moon
the hearts of all wanderers will dance forever!"

The Ritual

The wind's raspy voice called him back.
At the sight of an empty trash can
barreling and bouncing its way across the nearby road
then slamming into a parked car,
he regained his thrall, and with a big pull
yanked his steamer trunk in front of the full-length mirror.
Lighting a candle and stripping down naked,
his two hands namaste'ed to himself
as he bowed an honorable bow
to the smiling man in the mirror.

He remembered himself pious
and knelt at his altar.

The world-weary trunk seemed to explode as he opened it.
Handfuls of lacy fishnets,
jet black and firecracker red and elven green
with snappy garter attachments,
twisted through the air.
They were followed by a flirtation
of flapping leather chaps
and somersaulting sun dresses
and tumbling halter tops
and cheering culottes.
Molting flocks of escaping feather boas,
then batteries of bras
of every color under the rainbow, bounded out.

The air inside thrummed
with the spastic flurry of tweeds and plaids
and flattering stripes and smart, bright solids
until it looked like a tornado had busted up a Goodwill
and spread it across the landscape for the mercy of all.

WAITING ON THE MONSOONS FOR HIS DESERT SOUL

The scene outside matched the frenzy within
as loose papers and trash and leaves jostled about,
and small dead branches danced a last Tarantella across the yard
before even bigger winds came.

He guffawed,
thinking about how his Presbyterian minister father
would have had apoplexy
at his break down from moral composure—
let alone his reaction once he witnessed
his holy ark of sacred vestments.

The oft spoken refrain,
"You will dress with civility,
or you will suffer the lash for impropriety"
that had haunted most of his early years
now made him cackle all the harder.

He reached into the bottom of the chest
and grew a huge smile
as he dragged up his mother's brightly flowered hat box,
the wind outside now cackling as well.

Almost racing,
he girded himself in the black leather corset,
inching dozens of cross loops closer
until his chest felt close to collapse.
Cinching it tight until it became his skin
he admired how the bright red leather accents
carried a great complement to his heathen tan.

Then he slipped on tiny pink panties
too small to hold even a gherkin,
and he tucked ever so carefully.

Over this, several skirts of flouncy lace were applied,
a red one, then a yellow one, and then a teal green one on top.
He regally laid a hand-stitched

silk and pearl buttoned kimono over the corset;
golden chrysanthemums and royal peacocks
and gleaming pagodas screamed in vibrant ecstasy.
Leaving the front of the kimono open for view of the corset,
he wrapped a 6 foot long
sunflower-yellow Maribou boa around his neck.

He felt the picture coming into perfect focus.

Strapping on his roller blades,
he then steadied himself
as he carefully opened his mother's hat box
and lifted the contents into the air as if a gift from Heaven.
He held it aloft in praise
of the golden hued torpedo shaped felt form
with the brilliant pheasant plumes trailing far behind.
He coronated himself
as the man in the mirror gleamed in approval.

Closing his eyes in thanksgiving,
something hard and heavy smacked the window,
and he knew that it was now or never.

He grabbed the neon green goose-head handled umbrella
and rolled down the drive across the road
and over the short block to the bay front drive.
Stopping for one second to turn his hat around,
the feathers forward,
he moved into the center of the car-less expanse.
As he opened the umbrella
the strong wind from the incoming Hurricane Whitney
propelled him forward.

With two hands he held on tight,
the roller blades humming on the asphalt,
the gust billowing his stiff pheasant plume
and bobbing boa out ahead of him nearly horizontally.
Leaning his butt back for balance,

WAITING ON THE MONSOONS FOR HIS DESERT SOUL · 73

the giant bubble umbrella hauled him forward.

As the gusts lifted his frolicking skirts
he realized that all of his privates were now public,
and he went whizzing down the highway
with goddess as his co-pilot.

The last words from his mouth,
before the police
slapped "handsome wrist accessories" on him were,

"We come into this world naked; we go out the same,
and everything else is just drag."

The Last Performance

Outside the big top Huckleberry drifted into reverie,
the master of ceremony's last words to him still echoing,

"And now ladies and gentlemen
please join me in bidding a rousing farewell
to the unjoustable master joker of all jocularity,
the impeccable prefect of all pranksterism,
the consummate, unconquerable king of clown alley,
Huckleberry the Clown."

He merged into the mind twirl of that crowning moment.
Spiffendifferus had come toward him
into the center of the adoring crowd
to bestow a royal scepter,
a golden plunger on a six feet long silver handle.
Then, somehow, in quick turn,
five firemen clowns and their crazy hook and ladder truck
had barreled in to try and pry
the fakely suctioning plunger off his butt.
He kvelled at the remembrance of kids guffawing.

Inside the big tent the ebullient mc broadcast augustly,
"It's Road Runner Red, the Original Cowboy Juggler,"
while outside Huckleberry daydreamed
of his little cabin in the woods
in the Zuni Mountains waiting for him.
He had put all the extra money
he had had over the years into it,
bought the land, and built the cozy cabin for two
on the few weeks he had off each year.
He could feel the splendor of ponderosas,
beautiful sunsets, and vast starry skies.
"If only it were still for us two,"
he said softly to himself and cast his head downward.

WAITING ON THE MONSOONS FOR HIS DESERT SOUL · 75

The roar of the crowd inside
returned him to his reminiscence,
to the giant patchwork robe of neon green stitched together
and the orange polyester golf pants that boasted
purple fluorescent whales
and garrish pepto pink flamingos holding putters,
its long train flowing back yards behind him
and nearly out the tent's egress.
That's when the other clowns erupted.
A whistle blowing, clown car honking, riotous fanfare ensued
while the end of Huckleberry's robe was secretly, yet loudly,
hammered into the ground with yard long tent stakes
behind four clowns pretending to be a wall.
Huckleberry pretended not to notice what was happening.

Then Dipsy ceremoniously approached
with a magnificent golden crown on a satin pillow
held high in his hands.
Several feet away he tripped
and poured a host of confetti all over Huckleberry
from the crown which was in reality a secret pail.

He recalled the boom of hysterical laughter
from everyone in the audience
as the whole escapade deconstructed into chaos.
The clown truck erupted into smoke and flames.
Clowns tripped over each other,
falling into drums and fat ladies and pygmy goats,
collapsing upside down and oggly-gaggly
into the truck as it limped out.
And him, standing there
in his funny oversized pink and black pantaloons.
The breakaway outfit and the giant robe had broken apart
into twirling threads that sprang to life as he chased Dipsy
and the spikes held.
He laughed, shaking his head in joy and pride.

By the river, prancing elephants trumpeted effervescence.

His joy quickly shadowed to sadness,
"Oh my babies,
I will miss you so much!
You and I are dying breeds," he quietly said aloud.
His old bones felt truly tired.

Yet what he had once left behind,
what he had run away from,
what he was not allowed to have as a clown,
as a fool,
as a gay man,
as a nomad endlessly on the road—
all that he had willfully given up to be here,
felt possible again.
The yellow rose of sacrifice
he had pinned to his lapel
suddenly felt drab and hollow,
and he felt confused.

He wondered,
"Can old clowns ever die?"

But as bawdy barkers, cavorting crowds,
and bewildered, barking neighborhood dogs
formed this Fibinaci coded moment of his life,
a young girl approached
and offered him a giant sucker.
She said, "Huckleberry, I love you!
You make me happier than even my new baby sister."
As she hugged him,
the consummate clown let a tear escape from each eye.
And the never smearing makeup of the always-perfect fool
formed the cotton candy pink and blue sunsets
over the dark enchanting mesas in sacred snowclad silence
of his next clown capade.

And he knew the show must go on.

Metal

Her metal was the humanity
forged from the cosmic smithy's hammer.
Black castings of make-up, dress, and silence were her shields.
She would walk the coal train's straight and narrows,
setting pennies on the tracks.
Fascinated by their squashings
she would hammer them out even more,
drilling holes, and stringing them as amulets.
An antique skeleton key always hung
about her neck on a thick chain,
secretly waiting for someone to unlock her
from the lonely latchkey steeling of her youth.

Casting out the iron of her father's plans for her degree,
she majored in welding, sculpting, and folk dancing,
paying for it by painting
buxom bimbos on flame crusted frames
at the local Harley shop,
and winning armwrestling championships
at bars on state and national levels.

Pounded thin and drawn out wide
from the cauterizing of a failed marriage to an ex hell's angel
with a penchant for whiskey, other women,
and smashing her creations,
she ran silently in the night to a faraway town
to raise her three children alone.
Pouring her love into them as if they were bottomless vessels,
she stayed at home, fashioning clay seagulls and hammered goblets
for a local craft store.
In the endless rolling and pounding
from the disciplining, training, and adapting,
her once poor communication became honed,
her victim states dissolved into giving and receiving sharings.

An iron will developed into her sustenance.

Then, finally, a lustrous burnishment:
she married a Zuni Mud Goddess
in a lovely wedding on a Cape Cod beach.
She made a good living at her art,
especially by creating eccentric chastity belts and cod pieces.
She pounded copper and brass by hand,
then fastened coins, wheels, keys, razor blades, and other doodads
to them for different effects.
She retired to the Zuni Mountains in New Mexico,
creating giant metal sculptures on a three miles long art walk
and capturing award winning photographs
of sundogs, moonbows, and sideways lightning bolts on film.

She had become a good conductor of heat and electricity.

Empty Box Karma

A stiff wanting-wind
caught her unaware flapping
and tossed her façade of strength
high into the flippant-flow, hissy at her.
It swept her sky-bobbling dizzy,
and smacked her against the hard pack,
crushing the semblance of solid containment
that she once had held about herself.
The hot headwind drove her
along the scrubby path.
Under her, sharp fingers
snagged at loose trappings.
They tumbled her through the desert
of her willy-nilly abidance
where all the creations seemed to sport sharp pricks
for protection and control.
She felt most of those jag her to bleed,
but some hooked her up
and kept her around for a while.
They held her and nestled against her,
hooking her to their groundings,
whispering sweet ridiculousnesses into her ear.
But something always let go,
or swept her away,
and she would tumble along once more until she lay crumpled,
wedged in stone crevasse stillness
to bleach out and fray into cosmic flotsam,
contemplating her last in Carnation—

always the lost kid's face on her shirt
the last image seen,
haunting.

Captain

His early dreams always unfurled easily.
He caught drafts seemingly out of nowhere
that set him along his many fateful coursings.

He breezed along the coasts of academia.
He rose quickly from galley boy to first mate
on his early trimmings.
He swashbuckled his way to captaining his own destiny
while still a relative guppy to the rabid sharks
and the bloated whales eyeing him as krill.

But he was bolder, faster,
and much sleeker in his prevailing winds.
And his courtly talk above deck
came with cannons set to fire below the sight.
He captured many a booty with a wink and a hook.
He sailed the oceans of commerce like an old tar.

He played shell games
with his plucky disregard for failure
until the trumping pirates came,
and his holds were scuttled,
and his treasure stolen.
His ship beached on a bleached coral reef
in the parking lot of Treasure Island
in once ocean bottom,
now dry, Las Vegas.

His landlubber hatred pushed him.
He attempted new rigging,
but he had to put himself on lean rations.

He had to learn to harness his inner tempest
after the ballast from his haughty ego

WAITING ON THE MONSOONS FOR HIS DESERT SOUL

and his fixation on regaining paradise
drug him under his own ship from one side to the other
during his only tour of marriage.
The ill winds shredded what little
sail that was still sea-worthy.
He lived the rest of his life swabbing poop decks in paradise.
He found solace in desert squalls that rivaled the sea,
and once a day he would play
the Little Mermaid slot machine at the Bellagio,
willing for his ship to one day come in again.

The Seasons

(1)

The left eye of the small Navaho girl shot past him.
Frosted over like squalling snow blanketing all in white,
it chilled him.
When her bright right eye spied him,
terror and dread blanched this eye out as well.

He had come upon her family's car wreck
and saw her standing, shivering, staring at their brokenness.
He had come from behind
and placed a woolen blanket around her shoulders.
Her imprisoned eyes kept haunting him for days:
the blind one
and the fear fogged one
that called her to quickly toss off the blanket
after seeing who had put it around her shoulders.

His winter ended
to find his blue corn stash stolen by packrats,
kernel by kernel,
down to the cob,
except for twelve disciples still seated at the table.
He knew he must trust!

(2)

One day in late spring
he sensed a black leopard
around a Navaho woman who was seeking counseling.
He felt the large cat tickle the back of his throat
as it entered through his layers of consciousness.
With a rasping softness
a voice curled out to speak to the woman.

It advised her she must cross over salty waters
and release the shackle-held tears of blame that caged her joy.

Then the voice softened,
and a different energy took up space within him.
He somehow knew it was her son.
He heard the son tell his mother
that he did not want her to burden any longer.
He told her that she was not to blame for his death.
He told her that she must not reject her own true sweetness
by feeding her diabetes the only satisfaction she could find.

Her eyes rained,
then his.

He knew it was time to plant the corn again.

(3)

The relentless summer sun scorched his arroyo humor.
She who replenished did not even offer
tiny morsels from her virga pockets.
The no-see-ums seemed to seek him,
and the unseen seemed to clip the tether to his sacred tree.
The mad Zuni winds
continued to rattle his brittle foundations
as parched chipmunks nipped many a new sprout.
He shared precious collected waters with spare grace.

His new blue corn ached thirsty in its reaching.

(4)

The rain dancers drummed for three weeks solid.
Finally, the pleas were heard,
and the pocked lands
smoothed into ephemeral glistening lakes.

The corn rose up to touch the sky with their prayers.
The squash blossomed huge families
under sprawling canopies,
and the beans linked arms in hearty solidarity.

The cisterns and bellies and trust filled again.
A laughing contagion rang out, feeding all.

He joined the peoples in dance and song,

his blue corn pulsing a strong, sacred beat
from his feet to his heart.

Empire of the Son

Johnny's Uncle Bobby slept near to him as a child
in the same bedroom in twin beds only feet apart.
When Johnny remembered
what he would allow himself to remember
about Uncle Bobby,
his shoulders still hunched up to protect his neck
and rolled forward to protect his heart.
Resentments still bubbled from catalytic angers
and churned like toxic stew in his gut.
He recognized that he carried that response
for as long as he could remember
at the thought of his uncle's notice of his existence.

Uncle Bobby's legs were stiff and a little bowed
and, when he was in a hurry,
he reminded Johnny of how Brutus,
their family rooster, would run—
spindle sticks pistoning,
ruffled feathers flailing,
careening up to one's face to peck his beak askew
with rarely true accusations and blistering defamations.

More dreaded was the constant fear
of what corner Bobby would come cock-strutting around,
crotch-grabbing him like some teenage boy,
always managing to find a way to rub
some unctuous part against him,
talkin' trash about "needin' some fixin'"
and "headin' out to the henhouse"
with a slick wink at Johnny
and a rake of his tongue over his lips.
He never did this to anyone else that Johnny saw
and had no regard for their consequences—
except to make himself feel great again.

His sleazy Uncle Bobby's memory
kept regurgitating in him
as he witnessed Donald Trump's bid for the presidency.
He could only think,
"4 year olds who think they own the world,
shouting 'Me' and 'mine' and 'How great am I,'
need help to remind them
of how and when and why to share."

He hunched his shoulders
to think about what could happen next.
He wasn't sure where the adults were in the room,
but his child self
thought somebody needed
a good spanking by the universe.
Johnny's adult self could only shrug his shoulders.

A Mote of God's Eye

(1)

All along the golden-rayed way,
the evening tide's dazzling brilliance
plunged through the witness
of the narrow-slatted blinds.
They caught the sharp-edged motes of destiny
that swam on the waftings of his small breezes.

There was a time not long ago
that his relentlessness
blew the dust away from all things.
Life was about moving and doing,
creating, destroying, and recreating.
He rode the high winds of Brahma, Vishnu, and Shiva.
He once had been known by a thousand names:
"Gay Cabalero,"
"Filthy Tumbleweed,"
"Post-Apocalyptic Peter,"
"Eve of Destruction,"
and many others.
But he was happiest to be dubbed
"The Cosmic Firecracker."

He had never let any moss grow from face to face,
muse to muse,
lover to lover,
place to place.
The only flotsam allowed
was the dust which sometimes alit
upon his precious mementos.
They were his few sacred objects,
and it saddened him horribly to not see
their bright colors and luscious textures

sanctified in his sacred space,
helping to remember himself alive.

And he would laugh to himself
that the only thing he did more than traveling
was dusting.

(2)

Now he sits,
an older, slower man,
a finally made-to-root man.
Plunked among his ever-graying treasures
as the thronging castaways dip and dive and dance about him,
he recalls how disgusted he was for years
when he heard that dust was primarily the sloughing
of his and his fellow living creatures' skin and hair
and other secretions.
He revels in the fascination of when he had been told
that at any moment we breathe the molecules
of all beings who have existed.
He remembers the thrill
of thinking that he was breathing
Jesus and Buddha's molecular connections—

And then his gasp of horror
at the possibility of Hitler and Jeffrey Dahmer's dust
blowing in his inner winds—
all before he understood a choice-centered existence.

This time he sits enjoying flotsam's freedom,
the seeming-last movements
before Ever Changing Mystery
leads them to their next home.

Watching the lively chaos
slowly thin and swoop
and then begin to sweep toward

his newly cleaned soul confections
of sacred tchotchkes and esteemed heart treasures,
he feels more at peace with the thought
of his own light plunging through
the ever-narrowing slats of his own existence.
And so he decides
to sit more among the other celebrants falling
and enjoy the dance.
He knows he will less and less often
be able to clean,
or care about, cleaning them away
until he himself
becomes free, once more, to roam with them.

The Earth, the Fire, the Water, the Air, Return, Return, Return, Return!

Her air returned.
She took her seeds and germinated them
under moistened paper towels
under violet-ray-infusing hands.
She took a deep breath and channeled a soft chant
just an inch above them,
"Joy, peace, and abundance
to you and all your cousins!"
She rode a wave of ever-circling seasons with her breath.
She twirled under the full moon light at the swell of sowing,
spinning like a grouse in a sacred spiral dance,
in order to call power down and gently weave prosperity.
She planted her children in the early hours of the burgeoning
to make their birth an easy one,
and she cast a web spell of love
to the sparking sun and the assuring moon.

Her earth returned.
The gophers had come
and eaten the roots of much of the garden
in the harsh times.
She replanted most, but bore no ill will
as gophers helped to aerate the clotting soil,
and she believed they had a right to survive too.
She planted extra, knowing thirsty chipmunks
and squirrels would nip many a new young tender sprout
if she and her dog were not there minding.
She set out bowls of water and set a small plot of simple garden
a hundred yards outside her fence to offer back.
She believed she would always have enough.
She constantly worked to improve her own challenging soil.

WAITING ON THE MONSOONS FOR HIS DESERT SOUL

Her fire returned.
When she felt scared and vulnerable she went to her garden
and drank in the calming lavender.

When she was tired she lay down in the patch of sweet grass,
and her aches became unimportant
compared to the sweet grace of humanity
the grass always whispered to her about.
When she needed courage to face the day,
she would sit in astonishment at what had come up
through brick, hard clay soil, and impenetrable rocky blockages
with so little water to nurture
under an often brutal and torturous sun.
She would marvel at all that had still survived
the countless rabbits, deer, gophers,
mice, squirrels, chipmunks,
birds, insects, and other fellow creatures
that had just needed a little more to survive.
This always called forth her passion
and will to do what she felt she had to do
in the fuller garden of her life.

Her water returned.
She could always cry at the peonies.
They made her remember her mother
who seemed always to toil endlessly and complain bitterly—
except when she spied peonies,
returning her to fond childhood memories.
Then the peonies made her smile too,
and she counted them a miracle and a savior.
She would always sweat a good sweat,
a hearty 5 month sweat,
that bones and muscles were happy to ache for.
And when the monsoons came
she would laugh like a gypsy and weep like a saint at the same time.
She dropped her clothing
and outstretched her arms in receiving—
like the morning glory she sometimes thought herself to be.

If the roses pricked her
she would bleed a sacred drop back onto the ground
and cover it over.
She would pray for future generations of humans, animals,
and the earth they arose from,
to continue their sacred bond
of honor and connection with each other.
The sunflowers told her it would be so,
and she felt a great trust.

And her air came back round again.
Half her crop died from the early frost,
but she had plenty.
She took all the harvest stalks and stems and rotted offerings
and made a giant picnic spread of them
on the south side outside of the garden.
She noticed through the winter
that most of the gopher mounds led under the castoffs
and not into her treasures.

And she was pleased to co-exist.

A Dark Night of His Soul

A silent crusade of fog infests the shimmering dim,
lambent orbs of gossamer-shrouded streetlamps—
the masses huddle their eyes inside steel curtained stockades.
The night's river glides,
calling to lone rebels, ruffians, and rugged roustabouts.
Molasses monotones drone delinquently,
ruffling the blanket of the smothering stillness.
A strolling tranny strumpet
shadow trumpets solicitations.
The slow clop, clop, clop
of stiletto sharp palpitations on callous concrete
echo his lonely heartbeat
in her fading staging.
Gangs of melancholy
swarm in the passing shadows,
watching, with zombie allure, for apathy etched visages.
Hot cats clamor in clandestine coupling,
their torrid tempests scorching belly-up psyches.
They caterwaul away to unquiet nothing.
The utter silence swells to burst.
The advertising tap of the girl on her tour of duty
slashes through the sullen.
It trips the dullish din settled in,
only to again trail away into time's devouring vultures.

A Jealous Wind

Some have said that the wind is a jealous thing—
for it must always keep moving.
It can never just stop
and settle down with something or someone,
never has roots to say it belongs somewhere
or has ties to anything.
The wind must be a very lonely soul.
It seems it's always picking up company,
but only for a short while.

Jane lost her young son to the Iraq War.
Not so friendly fire, carried on the winds
of someone else's freedom-seeking, released him.
She enshrouded bullets he'd taken in her heart.
She eyed dandy lion puffballs with envy.

Flowers cloister their babies in sheltering petals,
fold close like mother's arms,
cup to collect nourishment, yes,
so that their children
won't be ripped from them before their time.

She had lost her daughter to no-named war
except the daily battle of living,
a precious bud smashed
by her own husband's brown thumbed hands,
a delicate blossom buffeted by his ill winds of selfishness.
He had plucked her up and battered her about
like a rose in a hurricane,
the hatred for those who didn't protect her now a prison
where she serves time in for murder,
the thorns of the thrashed rose the last structure standing.

A mother flower must somehow

just constantly let go into trust—
trust for when the tender wind caress turns tyrannical,
or the smooch of father sun blisters—
trust for when animals gnaw,
or humans trample,
or if the bees will kiss and share.

Reaching for the touch of the sun,
do they hold themselves back
because they may get burned?
If the rains don't come,
do they still find their bliss
knowing that their death
still feeds future generations of them and others?
Is there joy in knowing that the cycle will spiral on?

But some mothering part
will still always try to hold her babies close
until it's time to release them.

She changed her name to Zephyra:
drifted for a while.
No place felt like home.
Nothing made her smile
except a field of flowers in bloom on a windy afternoon.

Old friends say she became her name,
the gentle west wind always roaming,
picking up the broken children of flowers on the bloom
just to spend a little time
with those gone just too soon.

Another Trojan War

As a babe his mother dipped him
in lavender and patchouli,
then twirled him on a disco ball
to bless away his God infractions.
As a boy his father sent him
to a cadet school military:
"Make a man of my wimpy boy,"
one strong with no distractions.

He came to love the discipline:
found strength in self, confidence
to take on hard fought battles
and rise to conquer all.
He found the gem in sacrifice.
Duty fed his heart patience.
There was honor in just waiting.
One day he'd heed his inner call.

He joined the army, served his country:
lethal warrior, stoic soul.
Master Sergeant of the drill,
he set the cadence and the tone.
He made men follow to his rhythm,
made men step to his goal.
He sang the bonding in a brotherhood
of sweat and blood and bone.

Then one day he was out,
discharged, downbeat, and without sight.
His memory sparked of a place he'd heard about
in lonely, private whispers,
a place where men did things with men
to no Puritan's delight—
like dance together, love another,

call each other sister.

Off he ran to his world's smashing,
in and out of many covers:
men as soulmates, men as soldiers,
the lines of difference blurred.
Male, female, chaos, order,
in and out of many lovers,
his whole life's balance
seemed suddenly absurd.

So from dawn to dusk he drilled his blues,
donning some queen's high heels, borrowed,
on the well-beaten wooden dance floor
where the faeries took their meals.
Leaping, laughing, led giddy backwards,
"Nothing else as hard or hallowed
as the grace of surrender
needed in these *'I kill ease'* heels."

Dem Bones, Dem Bones, Dem Dry Bones

He was an ice age behemoth that lurked
behind a thin edged glass veneer,
a massive fragility plodding a petrified facade
barely holding past his constant fear,
a seemingly sweet and gentle soul easy to allay.
But above his head, if one chose to see,
angry storm clouds spat and stewed.
With random lightning bolts slashing
cross his left brow warning you,
"Run away! Wooley mammoth emotions stalk today."

The old ones used to tell him,
"Hide your treasures,
lash your back, and pray.
If you seem too pleased,
God will surely take it all away."

His father showed him
how to compete for money, fame, and love.
And in a brood of ten siblings
you either yelled above or shoved
if you ever wanted to be a twinkle in Dr. Daddy's distracted eye.
So he devoted himself to his books
until he feared his eyes would bleed
and he hustled to the call
to push and chase and lead.
But daddy only ever said, "You still can't beat my try!"

The old ones would tell him,
"You're here to weep and mourn.
Nothing good comes of being happy-born.
It won't get you somewhere better

once from this hell you're torn."

And so, he left home seething with a big,
"Fuck you, goodbye.
I'll show you all.
I'll make the call."
Mastodon feet stomp, but elephants don't cry.
So, he gathered words of knowledge
and claimed himself the know-it-all.
And he gathered words of spirit
and claimed himself the guru tall.
And he bellowed his mighty trumpet,
adding fake news to the pie.

He could still hear the old men tell him,
"Never let God see you smile;
pleasure's just the devil's play.
Love's impure thoughts rouse your fire;
God's anger will sweep it all away."

He struggled to let people in.
No matter how hard he tried
two-way streets could not compete
when one is filled with ruling pride.
His heart lay deeply walled, entombed in rigid thorns.
His life plodded along;
he could barely keep above
the rivers that threatened to capsize
a child's need for daddy's love,
a man still gored by ancient, thrusting horns.

The Old Ones always told him,
"Hide your love like a crocodile
behind sharp teeth that rip and fray."
Dinosaur bones can still be found
out walking in the gloom today.

On the Threshold

The timber-worn carpenter
stood at yet another of his door sills.
Feeling a slowing in his sap,
but still a primal urging ingrained,
he knew if there was a hole he had to build something in it.

And yet he paused.

His creaky, gnarled limbs throbbed
from the many devotions of his being.
There was an ache from the remembrances
of wrapping his loved ones in them tightly,
to the feeling of a fine hammer balanced.
There was a yearning from the power of a good day's work
with plum lines and honest squarings,
his latest creations
mirroring his many growth rings
in practice, patience, and perseverance.

Yet, he still could weep like willows
with the ache of those ripped out of his grasp.
He remembered the stunting years of many springs ago
when the taller ones took all the sun and most of the moisture,
but he had learned to sink his tap roots long,
and he had learned the patience that he soon would reach beyond
    them.

And he recalled the drought of a few winters back
when his roots didn't have soil around them,
and nothing and no one could clasp to him for he was too unsteady.

And the flood of 99 that came and took away his house
and his wife
and his joy in the sun.

He could still barely look back on that time.
He recalled his yellowing bark
and the loss of so many leaves and shoots.

But he had crawled out of his borehole and built a new house.
And new monuments had come.
And new love arrived.
And everyday devotions returned. And now a steady life.

But his sap felt like it was slowing.

He closed his woodened eyes to peer into the void,
past the portals of his door jamb reality,
and he envisioned his old bark and crumbling fibers
enshrined in a wooden box.

And he laughed, then wept,

then laughed again to silence.

On the Wire

He had always lived his life
traipsing a thin, taut edge high above the mundane.
By two he had climbed on every cabinet, sill, and table.
At ten he had found his way to the peaks
of the house, the barn, and the silo.
His anxious parents had pled, bargained, and cursed until blue
to get him to come down from places
before it got dark, and he fell asleep and tumbled off,
or before the lightning and wind took him,
or before the neighbors judged them to be horrible parents—
but his wild sheep heart always ruled.

He had broken most of his bones at least once
in his apprenticeship to mastering his surrenders
and his controls.

Surfing along the quantum wake
that defined ever-shifting form and fluidity
had taught him early that death
was often but an unfocused breath away.

He no longer had nightmares about
the freak fall ten years earlier
that had left him shattered
when his radar focus had been diverted
by a sudden unexplained flash
that had blinded him momentarily,
that had sent him toppling from the wire
to the ground fifty feet below
and an agonizing finale.

After many months of rehab,
when he finally could,
he had had to force himself to take that first step.

But he had hoisted his fear up the ladder,
hauled his less than agile limbs to his perch.
Once there the magician caught the charge
again because life was boring otherwise.
He knew he would rather
dance on a tight, thin rope he barely fit upon
than be numb on rock solid flatness.

He felt alive,
constantly putting one anchoring foot carefully
in front of the other,
breathing through whatever showed up,
and continuing to move no matter what.

He relished the ever-changing mystery of consciousness
hovering above the line that he could never focus directly upon.

His sage advice to others was that it was,
"Best to only hold
a soft caressing awareness
of both the total scene unfolding
as well as all of its meticulousness.
Too much thought confounds you,
and too little concentration stutters you into stumbling.

"If you are trying to make it look easy and believable
while always alert
to the sudden unpredictable gust of wind, unhinged cinch,
flip flopped prop, or frantic bird
suddenly lost and flapping wildly with you
at the top of the circus tent
ready to topple all, well,
that, to me,
is always worth life's price of admission."

The Baker

He was his own rising in the middle of the night,
softly slipping out of bed
as his wife dreamed on downy turnovers.
He kindled the fire in his belly with some good Viennese
and one of yesterday's Scottish scones
while he stoked the big kitchen oven to dragon breath.
He felt his heart's yeast burgeon
at the golden dawn glazed onto the mountain.
Morning loaves cooled on the racks,
their enticing aroma ubiquitous.

Today his first customer was a croissant.
He always had fun imagining his clientele
as the goods they bought.
Her refined elegance supported a risen above air.
Only the finest ingredients and choicest cuts would satiate her.
Her kneads were long flowing strokes pampered
and fed plump by the rich cream skimmed from the top
and massaged over and over
into a luxurious silken pillow haughtiness.
But the baker knew
one takes a lot of beatings,
and goes through many chillings,
and the fire is always hot no matter what
to just be a loaf of bread,
let alone a perpetually pummeled
gout-poppin', high fallutin' croissant.

His next was a thin bread stick man
meagerly living on mere morsels of sustenance.
He was tall and salty like the sea he plied for most of time.
His teeth had all but vanished to John Paul Jone's locker.
Three-day old bread sticks dipped in thin chicken stock gruel
were now the essence of his sailing.

He served some plain cake people with too sweet frostings.
They were headed home to hunker down
to TV and cheese doodle meanderings.

A dozen minus two chocolate chip cookies came in
with their random bike keys and latest internet gadget
and skateboards and books.

The mean biscotti woman stormed in,
beating her stiffness against the counter,
demonstrating about the nuts that were too hard
and the fruit too gummy.

He was happy he was a muffin.
He had a life full and round.
It was not too sweet, but rich enough.
And he cherished his plenty of irregular size holes
to fill with meaning and interest,
along with his wife, the sour cream apple pie.

Feeding people's bellies and souls was his just dessert.

The River

(1)

For most of his life
he never knew the hours before dawn.
He never felt the mystery of it,
the surrender it required,
the ripening in it.

He could never wait.
As a kid he would sneak around for weeks prior,
opening hidden Christmas presents
and then meticulously rewrapping them beyond suspicion.
But not only would he open his,
he would open everyone's.
The thrill of knowing beforehand tasted luscious.
It was juicy like the pomegranates and wine
grandma always secretly horded in her closet,
extra juicy like the stack of Inches he found one year
tucked away under all the ammo in his dad's private gun cabinet.
And despite his anger and confusion at times,
just the knowing was always a hidden gourmet pleasure.

Every Christmas Eve
found him with a smirk like a demented elf
while he clutched some exquisitely adorned box to his bosom
like a jaguar's mouth on prey
and secreted it away to his lair's bedroom closet.
There, like a forensic specialist, he would dissect it
precisely to find its bones
and then reassemble it with the same agility and finesse,
every river of curling ribbons
still waterfalling as brilliantly as before,
every folded edge still crisp and sharp.
There were no extra creases, tape pulls, or off center anything.

It was the real McCoy's authentic replica of wrapping.
Then he would replace it in the exact same place as before
and steal another away to the titillating thrall of exposure
until all unknown was known.
He would be asleep before dawn
with no more exhilaration left toward any divine mystery,
and then, every Christmas morning,
the practiced surprise "Oh mys,"
the mirror toned round mouths,
and the wolf in doe wide eyes of astonishment .
The thrill would last for weeks.

(2)

But he made a promise to himself
that he would never use the knowledge gained to hurt anyone.
He learned that lesson
when his poor brother was caught with an ounce of pot
as a result of his own jettison of a tongue to a friend.
That betrayal then bled hot to his mother
and surge-channeled back to his father
who threatened castration, incarceration, and excommunication.
He hated his father's hypocrisy.
He wanted to speak out in his brother's defense,
but his own hypocrisy leveed him to silence.

(3)

It took him many years
of trying to push the river to find some peace.
It took him many years
of yanking oysters from their shells
before their pearls were fully formed.
It took him plying the waterways
of many loves and several marriages
with many double crossings and plank walkings
and other high seas dramas along the way.
It took him many courses of passion to find his stream

from actor to detective and then to honest carpenter.
It took him sprouting and growing children
along the banks of life
to deepen channels of connection and honor
and to heal his deepest trenches.

Finally, could he recognize the beauty
in rising before Christmas Day's dawning,
to see the trees without leaves
standing naked against the newborn sky,
to feel their patience in their waiting with a great trust
that the old is gone
and that the new leaves will start growing
in the right course and time.
It took him many years
before he knew life's sacred, eternal juices,
before Christmas presents
were replaced with Christmas presence.

BOOK III

MY AUTHENTIC LIFE

The Formative Years

Encampments of small men often surrounded him.
Daily he spread their lives across living room sofa mountains,
shag plains, countertop mesas, and stainless-steel sink lakes.
A Lincoln log cabin would grow up in one place,
nearby a metal, bright red barn with façades of windows painted on.
Farm animals teemed in every state of lambing, ramming,
meowing, mooing in attached corrals.
Neoprene powder blue all male farmhands
carried buckets, slopped hogs, hoed fields.
Bowlegged all beige cowboys straddled horses
as far as the eye could see.
Their lassos twirled forever in the air.
Some had pistols always poised to shoot.
They herded cattle grazing on shag rug fields.
Others aimed long rifles at deer crossing the strata lounger plateau.
Across the way
an Indian village of white teepees, dogs,
and various colored horses thronged.
A great camp of buff, shirtless, breechcloth-clad all red men poised in
    tableau,
some with bows set with arrows shooting at some unknown essence.
others astride their ponies leading off on hunting parties,
all in strong proud stoicism,
the story yet to unfold.

He exhausted hours and hours standing up little wobbly action
    figures
on multitudes of frustratingly uneven surfaces,
breathing through constant teeterings and topplings
that would knock over scores of people—
all needing to once more be set upright.
Then, finally, he could sit in amazement at the final creation
of teeming life in still motion:
a Virgoan beauty found in the patterning,

a swollen joy and pride in the wealth from will and toil,
a peacefulness in the vignettes of co-existence without chaos or
    mayhem.
Then his stories would unfold and countless movements of men
    ensue.
But he took the most pleasure
from the erection of his dream setting for the day.

Often his older teenage brother,
for the many years he created life in miniature,
would swarm through the genesis.
He would drag his feet in broad swathes,
smashing pillows on whole camps,
then laugh mockingly as he ran away,
giddy on the resultant horror and rage.
Once more that would return him to rebuilding his dream,
cursing at his brother.

He smiled
remembering the last times he played with those men.
He must have been about 10 or 11.
He couldn't remember any of the stories any longer,
but the one image that still stood out vibrantly to him
was that his best days often ended with the cowboy and the Indian
riding off together on the same horse,
their bodies cuddled against each other in the saddle
as they rode off into the sunset:
Happy trails,
without a clue to what it would mean in his life.

He Didn't See That Coming!

Closeted farm boy
shot his first and only buck at 17—
stared dispassionately into its wide stiff eyes
afraid that he felt nothing.
He called his older brother to gut it
and then soaked it for 12 hours in red wine and red onions,
cast it as fluffy swiss steak swimming in gravy seas,
curried it into tender flank pounded thin
laid with prosciutto and carrots and rolled to *braciola*.
He crammed mixings of it with Parmesan and anchovies
and peppers and stems into giant mushroom caps
baked in white wine and butter,
and blended even more of it
into a fragrant four cheese and spinach lasagna.
Then he called his unwitting friends to come to a feast.
12 devouring friends came in a feeding frenzy.
He came out, dancing around the table,
with the 7-point rack on top of his head.
Someone asked, "What's that?"
"What you're eating!" he replied.
The 6 kids from cities screamed, "No!"
One moaned, "Bambi."
6 abruptly got up and drove away.
The 6 from the country just kept on eating.
He didn't see that coming.

Shivering from normality he ran away to pan for gold,
but April's Rocky Mountain rivers were still frozen.
Running out of gas in Waco Texas,
he abandoned his Volare in the Walmart parking lot
and took off hitchhiking.
Suddenly he found himself robbed of all he had and stranded.
For 3 weeks journeying on the roads in the desert southwest,
he survived on the kindness,

and tried to avoid the strangeness, of others.
A sandstorm nearly felled him,
left him cowering in a culvert,
sand in all his cracks.
But an old-fashioned traveling dog and pony show,
wind battered and weary too,
welcomed him to her roustabout nation.
And, suddenly, there he was in clown makeup
and giant oversized clothing,
fake moose antlers bobbling off his head.
He didn't see any of that coming.

After five vehicles blew up underneath him
he ran away from the circus
to suddenly join his first gay friendly town
where the queers weren't hidden under outrageous costumes
because they just openly wore them.
A boyfriend moved in with him,
stayed for three months in his tight but functional apartment.
The boyfriend called him one day, telling him to take the bus
out to the other side of the island
to meet a realtor to show them a possible cute new place.
He waited at the Wal-Mart bus stop for two hours.
No boyfriend, no realtor.
He went home to find the boyfriend
had packed his stuff and slipped away.
He felt like a deer awestruck in headlights:
didn't see that one coming either.

He fell asleep one night from anti-itch pills
and woke up to find that someone
had shimmied up the giant banyan,
scaled over his second floor balcony,
snuck in while he slept,
rooted around just inches from his head,
took his beaver skin fedora,
some of his toiletries,
all of his gold chains and charms, a six pack of coke,

and a very large oil painting of a tree
that he had put 40 hours into
and was only half finished with.
But they left his cash, his camera,
and a whole bunch of other dear stuff
that he thought a true robber would also want.
He felt dirty and abandoned again.
Could never have planned for that one either.

But these kind of odd events were just the beginning.
And after 58 years of continuing odd situations,
a certain calmness and surrender prevailed.
They made great stories after all was said and done.
He was no longer one to just muddle in the mundane
because he never knew just what the hell might happen next.

Your Children

A long way into a chosen life of adventure
some would covet and others pity,
Kahlil Gibran's suddenly found words
had sparked him with encouragement.
They allowed him to look back at the wonder and awe
and find trust in his path again.
Your children are not your children.
They are the sons and daughters of life's longing for itself.

He thought of the spur, a teen rebellious angst
at being denied his own beliefs.
He was angry at only feeling allowed to be other people's ideas
of right and proper and good and smart.
He pined for relief from chafing chains of constraint
where even simple challenges led only to threats
and public humiliations
and protective coves of silence,
and so, one night, he secretly slipped away
to another corner of the country.
They come through you, but not from you
And though they are with you they belong not to you.

And he began to live truer to himself,
but still his closets were overstuffed.
And he lived more lovingly to himself,
but still his tongue lay mute.
And he lived freer with himself,
but still his heart lay bleeding, empty.
And he awoke one day, not that long afterward,
to find he had again sold his soul to a money-making,
spirit-starving, other people's life-on-production-line of being.
You may give them your love but not your thoughts
For they have their own thoughts.

And he remembered his sudden thrill
when, on April Fool's Day of 1979, he had leapt
through the fantastic folly of his lonely heart
to pursue the gold that might bring joy—
and how the icy, racing rivers numbed him to pleasures,
and bone chilling sluicing,
was like the tearing open of his own soul—
and how along the path he was stripped of everything
and windblown to nothingness for a long time
until he thought that he, too,
had begun to understand the suffering of the world,
and how the path he was on had begun to make some sense.

He thought back to the lonely snowy morning
when he called his mother on his twenty-third birthday
after disappearing nearly two years prior.
He felt again the queasy churnings of shame and fear tossing
that combined with need and joyful anticipation.
How desperate he had been to find himself!
Running away from his many small-spirit confinements,
running with all his real truths kept locked within his prison of fear,
a stitched-on smile had been his armor
and the entrance to his jail cell for as long as he could remember.
Escape and running away dangled the only key to any chest of hope,
and truly, he thought, his only chance at happiness.
And so he had run away.
You can house their bodies, but not their souls.
For their souls dwell in a place of tomorrow
that you cannot visit, not even in your dreams.

And when he called on his 23rd birthday
and told his mother he was a clown in a circus,
he remembered her words—like a prison's stale old bread and water.
She cried to him that they had had a private investigator
trying to find him for over a year.
She told him she worried that the neighbors
and church judged her as a bad mother.
She told him to come home,

that she couldn't stand the fear of him being alone on his own,
and that she worried that the fear would kill her.
He remembered he told her,
(he thought kind of like Jesus told his mother Mary),
"I love you,
but I must stay on my path."

And then he thought about his father and mother coming to see him,
a garish clown on a tiny circus lot in desert-sun blistered Arizona,
and his father saying to him,
"I give up trying to tell you what to do,
I only want you to be happy,"

and he laughed to think
that he hadn't yet even told him that he was gay.
He smiled at how far he'd come along his path
and how much more he'd romp and prance
on his merry adventures as a gypsy faery wizard.
You may strive to be like them, but seek not to make them like you—
For life goes not backward nor tarries with yesterday.

The Bittersweet Sound of Old Trains Whistling By

(1)

"Nana had a bad day today!"
An oft-stated phrase etched into my mind-plate,
Mom saying it as I returned one day from high school:
"The Hoffmans found her naked…
down by the railroad crossing."
Her voice frustrated,
her eyes darting, but never landing on me.

My grandmother and trains are indelibly linked.
My earliest memories are of her and me hand in hand,
walking along the tracks
just beyond the bottom of our hay field,
waving at engineers slowly creeping by
on the curvy country run.
And of picking bushels of elderberries
that just loved that track-bed lava reflected heat.
Sometimes we would cross over the tracks
to go to our favorite little crick pond below
to find where the perfect round brown mushrooms
were against certain sides of particular trees.
We would bring them home,
and she would fry them up for breakfast
with morning eggs from our coop
for the two of us and Rock.

One day in my early teens Mom's statement was different,
and our lives changed.
"Your dad had a bad day today!"
The story told me that my grandmother
had come out into the living room that morning

with soiled underpants.
She took them off
and flung them down the living room steps
and against the front door wall,
gone from her sight and smell and concern.
So, my father,
returning from a day burning steel
to work on the family farm,
saw a brown patch on the wall.
He wondered where chocolate would have come from
and stuck his finger in and brought it to his nose to smell.
Bad day on the farm!

(2)

The stories I grew up with about her always amazed me.
My Nana was 13
when she was forced into an arranged marriage.
She came to the new world
with her 30 years old husband, Dominic.
I was told stories of his being an angry man,
an often self-righteous man
who could curse his life with great torment,
would administer harsh repercussions to his sons
for their transgressions,
would snap cow's tails in fits of rage:
agony screaming through the farm
as yet another cow with a lightning bolt shaped tail
bellowed his reputation around the county.
But he never hurt her, I was told.

She married her childhood sweetheart,
but not until she was 64 and Dominic had passed.
Her beloved Rocco, her Italian childhood boyfriend
followed her to America back in 1903
and had worked on the railroad
and lost a leg to it
and limped on a wooden leg with a cane.

I knew her then, with Rocco.
She was still alert before Alzheimer's took her last 30 years.
She would still dance
and talk mostly in Italian, which I didn't understand,
and work tirelessly at gardening and cooking.
My favorite memory was of her comforting me on her lap
while watching Bonanza, Polka Varieties, and Lawrence Welk.

When I was 19, and she 77,
I remember finding her upstairs
searching frantically for Dominic (her first husband),
25 years gone.
Rocco was now 5 years gone.
She was searching anxiously
for the two bushel baskets of chestnuts
she said Dominic had put in the cellar.
Or so I made out from her mostly Italian monologue,
not seeing me,
not recognizing that I existed just two feet away from her,
looking through the eyes of another time.
I watched her become frustrated,
then call for Jesus to take her hand and come to bed,
and off she went,
her hand holding Jesus's.
She had caught a much different train..
I remember sad tears laying tracks down from my eyes.

(3)

Today,
train whistles in the distance
still stir golden memories
of chasing ducklings and turkey babies
around her dining room floor.
And of talking to the scary ghosts
in her bedroom closet with her.
She taught me to roll meatballs and bread pretzels,
feasted me on an ever-present cornucopia

of native and Italian succulence.
She hated my mother's "bland" English cooking;
she would sneer at her and call her cruel names
under her breath, fortunately in Italian.
Another indelible memory arises
of sitting outside the farmhouse, Rock, Nana, and me.
He played a lively tune on his handmade wooden flute.
She bounced me on her knee,
laughing at the dance,
adoring the songbirds singing along in the trees.
She loved the "jayluts" (little jays birds).
She loved me, "Raphaluts" (little Ralph bird), the name she called me
when I began to sing along.
A train in the distance
always seeming to be whistling along too.

Those last 30 years were hell on my family.
She had a ticket to ride from what they called
hardening of the arteries back then,
and she boarded completely
soon after Rock no longer anchored her.
Jesus had been her life-long companion
and became her main traveling mate in the end times.
He had comforted her through the years of the "brute,"
who once had grabbed his first son's wife's hand
in front of his second son's wife (my pregnant mother)
and shoved it down into his pants.
That event set off a firestorm of rage and fists
and rest-of-life-long bad blood between father and sons.
I think he had senility too!

Through her last 20 years,
she would lay a handkerchief perfectly squared
next to her on her bed,
and there, baby Jesus would lie.
On the other side of her in her narrow twin
lay another handkerchief,
perfectly squared, for adult Jesus.

Fortunately, she was only 4'10" and 99 pounds, so there was room on the train's narrow sleeper.

In Training

He would hide in his Nana's camphor choked closets
among the pressed grays and blacks
and the flower print smocks,
and even though the ghost in that closet scared him,
he still hid there.
The poking and prying specters
on the other side of the keyhole
haunted him more.

He would hide in secret straw forts in the massive hay barn,
going from cozy den to cozy den through narrow, scratchy tunnels
if the grenades of criticisms were exploding in his home.
He silently would skirt chicken coop walls
to avoid the verbal conflagrations
always erupting between two hard of hearing,
and angry as viper, brothers
that spilled out and over onto children
and wives and other animals.
He would creep like a cornered mouse
into corncribs and old horse stalls,
avoiding the noxious cow barn if he could
and run to the orchard to hide in an apple tree
if he really had to.
The blasts from fiery furnaces were too hot
to willingly just stand and be scorched by the flames.
He would hide behind closed eyes,
pretending to be unavailable just as a general precaution.
He was a convincing sleeper.

Years later he would understand
that he too had post-traumatic stress disorder
from his often-seeming world at war youth.
He would realize that many of the old evasions
still plied his quiet waters.

He would laugh, thinking that he would have made a great spy if his queer authenticity wasn't so important to him.

Happy Father's Day

Great bald head, dark as a hickory nut,
browned by the blazing sun of countless hours, days, years
of hay baling, barn building, and the tending
of black angus, chickens,
and at least one stubborn child
who swore he did not want to be like you.
Great Italian nose,
hawk-like, swooping,
eternally stuffed with the chaff
from corn, wheat, oats, sod, and particulates of the steel
burned and brazed in the factory
at your other full-time job— always a handkerchief upraised
to catch the mass of putrid gumminess
that broke free with a grunt and a boom—
always a great glottal dredging up of phlegm
to expectorate at the ground,
regardless of who was around.
Great singing voice,
rarely shared except in quick little ditties or forced Sunday psalms,
that, not often enough, lifted me out of myself
enough to appreciate you.
Great anger,
that seemed to scream too often from your mouth,
eating away at you
and handed down to me.

So much never seemed to work the way that you wanted it to,
or people to do as you wished,
and very little seemed to please you.
You would say, "Never trust anyone,
because everyone will stab you in the back."
I rarely seemed to please you,
or do enough for you,
or lead the life that you wanted me to.

You called me "stupid," "fat," "lazy," "worthless like an old woman,"
"lacking in common sense," "a stubborn jackass,"
among so many others.
You tried to force me to play baseball
when I wanted to do anything else.
I remember sitting in left field,
pulling hands full of grass from the earth
and tossing them over my shoulder
as fly balls zipped over my head.
You cursed and mocked me
and threw the demise of myself and the world at me,
but finally stopped trying to make me play baseball.
Yes, I was a stubborn jackass!
I was a gay boy hiding for my life.

I judged you my great torturer.
I crept along barn walls, ran to the woods,
slunk silent in hay tunnels, behind the couch,
anywhere to escape your bombastic pronouncements
of disdain and abhorrence.
You, born of a father
who I heard was equally as verbally violent as yourself.
You, born of a father who was physically violent as well.
My grandfather who, in fits of rage,
would go out and crank the tail of one of the cows,
snapping and twisting it into a gross deformity
as the poor creature wailed in agony.
Your father,
who reportedly sometimes treated his sons equally as harshly,
was a county-wide legend,
because of the farm of cows all with contorted tails.
And yet, you, Dad,
never laid a hand on me in a violent manner.
Thank heaven for evolution.
And once in a while
you would sweep into the kitchen as Mom cooked dinner,
and you would grab her and hug her,
kiss her and dance her around the floor.

I would watch with amusement and embarrassment
as you would sing and laugh and prance
like some alien had stepped into your body and taken over.
And sometimes
you would share a box
of your favorite candy, black licorice, with me,
or vanilla milkshakes that you would whip up for us.
And occasionally
you would break away from the demands of survival
and come and see me in a play,
or in a concert singing.
Only after your death did I learn
that you raved about me to your friends
even though you never seemed to appreciate me to my face,
only exhorting me to do better, be more.
And long after I had chosen not to be the doctor,
or dentist, or lawyer that you pushed me to be,
and instead studied psychology,
and then became an assistant chef,
then a carpenter's apprentice,
then a circus clown,
finally, then, did you say,
"I give up trying to make you something else,
I only want you to be happy."
And only then did I consciously start to love you again;
only then did I begin to witness the rage and grief
in my heart and the emptiness in my own soul.

And then, suddenly, you died
from your burning steel:
too soon for me to come to know you,
too soon for us to maybe become friends,
too soon to see you relax into retirement and enjoy your life,
maybe for the first time.

And yet now,
when I have taken the chance to ask you for support,
you have appeared to me in my dreams,

reaching out and hugging me.
Or you have sent me serendipitous fortune.
I know it!
That's when I realize that you have loved me all this time,
even when I judged you,
hated you, feared you, longed just for a kind word from you.
All the times when I thought I was alone, friendless, unlovable,
I realize finally that you just wanted me to be
a well-rounded, healthy, happy, intelligent, and capable man.
Not to satisfy your ego,
but to give me a life
that you believed was never fully offered to you.

One more remembrance,
of that beautiful singing voice that I too rarely heard.
After you died, mom said that you really only sang
when you were in pain
because it helped to ease that pain and to rise above it—
and that the greater the pain, the louder you sang.
She told me that in your final days
your song was constant and deafening.
I can still hear you sing "Amazing Grace,"
and I am still moved to tears.

Death By Pink

It almost always scared him,
that color pink.
To wear it in high school
opened one to the wink,
the insinuations,
the namings,
the houndings,
the stink.

A whistling lisp of "esses"
pushed his fear of the link.
Clumsy and awkward,
mocking jocks dished his sync.
His closet held secrets
that could land him dead or in the clink.
"They" said he had a disease
or his soul was jinxed.

So, sometimes,
he would cower like a skink
at the thought of wearing anything
with even a touch of pink.
When the courage it took
to unwind the fearsome chink
that writhed around the simple act
might take him to the brink.

He had to gird his loins
and cast his spell of re-think.
"I must be stronger
than the snickers, laughs, and winks,
stoic to the punches
that have made me wince and blink
from someone feeling threatened

by a man sporting pink.

But there's far too many cups
from which I must take a drink.
And there's far too many loves
with whom my heart links.
And there's far too much unfairness
to not give voice and ink
to let a little color make
my courage sink.

And little by little
he stepped through the stink,
welcomed the world
into more of his kink.
And found the youth of our country
barely even blink
at a faggot getting through
his fear of death by pink.

Disciplined Wild One

He found enthrallment
from his chaste demand to understand layers,
gingerly unwrapping the casing
of semi-hard chocolate shell frosting.
He would try to pull it off in one contiguous sheet
and gently lay it on a plate.
Then he would carefully peel apart the mystical spiral
of thin chocolate cake cuddled
against the thick sheet of thickened sweet cream.

Secretly and slowly,
he would feed himself the floppy run of delight
like a baby bird being fed a worm by its mama.
Then, delicately,
he would fold the thin, luscious outer coating
into his communion wafer,
set it on his tongue
with eyes closed in reverence:
to melt and to remember.

He found balm in them when he feared his father
had lost affection for him
for not doing what daddy said he should do,
or for being one more of many things
that daddy said he shouldn't be.
He found solace stuffing his face,
in rapid succession, with one after another
with no pretense of ritual
until nauseous from the host of HoHos
hidden in the closet of his youth.

In his life he would have many closets.
There would be many pleasureful
as well as pain-giving things

that he would hide in them.
He came to understand that they were often trying
to fill some sweetness he felt missing in his soul.

But they also came to show him
many layers of understanding along the way.

Blessed be to all paths.

Free At Last

(1)

His cracked open egg-soul fried in the beating down heat.
Adventure seared his smiling, cracked lips.
Freedom scraped against his scorched red shoulders
hunched without other people's "shoulds."
The power to choose chaffed his butt,
brought twinges to his hamstrings,
and cramped his soleus,
but he was happier than he had been in a long, long time.
Aloneness, the sound of two bike tires whirring,
mesmerized him into his highway humping beat.

(2)

The first day
the South Carolina coastal highway nearly killed him.
Every tree was a massed corsage of flowering beauty
along the humid, swampy forest.
Intoxication funneled up his nose
with the 10-mph headwind he struggled against.
A pounding headache came on at about 40 miles.
His legs throbbed with pain at about 45 miles.
At about 50 miles his stomach churned.
The sun scorched great swathes of his body
and blistered his shoulders, forearms, and upper legs.
He collapsed into his tent at early evening,
threw up his lunch,
and passed out from the relentless burnings of the day.
A miserable night sleep followed.

(3)

The second day seemed endless.

Everything ached to the beat of limbs
endlessly pumping against blistered skin.
No amount of sunscreen and aloe cooled enough.
The searing, will-sucking oppressiveness of it all
nearly made him turn back.
He pushed on, the price to his spirit too hard for surrender.
He made it 100 miles on the second day;
a cooler headwind helped a little,
Virgo doggedness the main dictator.
He collapsed just before sunset
and slept, fitfully, behind a billboard on a fairly quiet road.

(4)

A panic attack on the 3rd day
froze his body at the top of the Charlestown bridge.
He had mistakenly taken the wrong bridge,
the one without a pedestrian's walk.
He had made it up the steep bridge,
walking his bike carefully up the narrow arm
along the busy lunch hour rushing two-lane.
He made it to the top and pulled into the slightly wider pull off.
But he couldn't go down the other side.
His heart raced to see the steepness.
His breath labored as he tried to see
how he could get down any way at all.
His third-degree sunburn on his shoulders screamed at him,
and he just wanted to cry.
He stood for ten minutes, desperation choking,
when an open bed truck hustled to a fast stop within inches of him,
a woman shouting, "Throw your bike in back and get in quick!"
The kindly nurse had passed him once before and seen his angst.
She had turned around twice to fetch him to safety.
He thanked her endlessly on the short drive
and hopped out at the bottom.

He made another 100 miles that day by riding into the night.
It held a surreal haze straight through Georgia,

straight through a moonless eeriness,
straight through the endless small towns of seemingly all black folks,
drinking on their old car roofs outside their shack homes,
dancing to juke box boogie on broken sidewalks,
clapping, shouting, partying
while he,
closeted gay boy,
dressed in white hooded sweatshirt,
hood up because it was chilly,
pumped hard and fast in possibly dangerous territory.
He kept thinking, "I hope they don't think I'm KKK on a bike,"
ashamed that he felt so racist, but still so damned scared.

(5)

The fourth day he found a wallet along a beach,
stared at it for minutes,
took the $265 in cash he found in it,
placed it in a mail box.
He felt so poor and hungry.
He ate well,
but the guilt and shame ate right back at him.

(6)

The fifth and sixth days were Florida ocean beauty
mixed with relentless torrential downpours and exhausting humidity.
But evenings were remarkable, cool and welcome.
Guilt and aches and burns still plagued him, but he could still smile.
He slept in a 1976 bicentennial fort
that had been abandoned for nearly three years.
Something kept snuffing on the other side of the wall all night.

(7)

The seventh day
he was nearly hit by a van that had the choice to either take him out
or hit the old man who had blindly crossed the fast highway

on his doddering bike
to visit the young man changing his tire in the median.
The sheriff and ambulances and others stopped at the ugly scene
where the van had smashed the old man and bike into a tangled
    heap
just a few feet in front of him.
He was stunned as the driver had only missed hitting him by a foot.
After answering questions and watching for a short while,
he got back on his bike, still in shock.
He rode 1 mile before he realized his tire was flat again.
He rode 40 more miles until a bunch of teens on a corner sidewalk
made no pretense at showing they wanted to take his bike from him.
As he sped away he knew, at that moment,
he couldn't go any further.
He called a taxi to take him the last 60 miles to Miami.
The 19 years old's adventure had shook him to his core.
"Freedom," he suddenly thought,
"does not come easily or without responsibility,"
shrugging his blistered shoulders and soul.

Rocket Man

(1)

Old Man,
why did you do that, sir?
Suddenly cocking your rickety bike at a 90 degree angle,
you turned off the roadside
and pushed straight toward me.
I watched your hardworking, wobbly legs
make a big bumble beeline toward me.
Your eyes were transfixed.
I saw gladness stretch from ear to ear
while you rode straight into the path
of that brown van cruising down the inside lane
of that active afternoon highway.

I remember the driver's bulging eyes
as you and he swept by 10 inches from me.
He was a young man whose long brown hair
framed a horrified face
stuck to a soundless scream.
He seemed to have no time, no space,
no karmic destiny, but one:
to catch you up, Old Man,
like a locomotive's cow catcher,
to pitch you and your bike
with a thwacking, bone-cracking squish
up against his passenger-side grill and windshield.
I felt that impact as your twisted body pretzeled with your bike
and slammed against that van's face.

(2)

These many years later, Old Man,
that experience still exists vividly in my continuity.

You had one shoe blown completely away,
and your brown sock flew halfway off
like a windsock catching a stiff breeze.
The back of your skull was embedded against shattered, solid glass.
I remember it framed your alabaster countenance
in a weird luminescent, cracked glass halo.
You looked almost angelic with your eyes rolled toward heaven,
and you had a cock-eyed smile,
broad and bright and surreal,
juxtaposed against that driver's silent face, cringing horror.
You reminded me of Dr. Strangelove riding
on the nose cone of a rocket blasting into space.

Both of you rushed by me,
the van only 10 inches away as it slammed on its brakes.
I could have touched you.
Your and his faces were etched in metal and glass.
You and your bike crumpled to the ground
in front of the stilled brown beast.
I can remember that I stood immobile,
in stunned disbelief as traffic stopped,
as sheriffs converged,
as ambulances wailed,

and then when the young driver came over to talk to me
and told me that he had had to make a decision
when he saw both of us in front of him.
He said there had been a car to his right
and palm trees to his left
and the two of us in the middle.
"I had nowhere else to go.
It was either take out the old guy,
or take you out."
He added with a heavy sigh,
"So I chose him."
I can still feel my shock from his statement.

(3)

Thank you,
you brought me many lessons, Old Man.
And often I remember your face,
bliss-filled figurehead on the prow of your embarking vessel.
And I now believe that you were out,
free, and in bliss.
You cracked the egg,
broke the yoke,
slipped the coil,
and spiraled out into cosmic absorption.
There was no pain on your face,
only a sublime, but quirky, ecstasy.
Pumped and primed,
straddling your rocket,
you roared off in a grand salute.

I have wondered if life had seemed fair or unfair,
good or bad to you?
But you seized that day and eclipsed the sun.
You sent pangs and promises of humanity
rippling off in all directions
throughout my time and space
to weave anew the threads of illusion and reality.

And I am humbled.
You have often reminded me
to treat life with utmost respect and gratitude—
for any second could be the last.
You tell me to slow down
in my hurry to get to the next thing.
And you have quickened in me
the spirit to ride the winds of change
with passion and trust and a smile on my face
and a sharing of grace.
And, I believe,
that I assisted in your transition

and that you, too, relied on me—
as you have assisted in mine.
I feel honored and privileged
to have danced that last tango with you, Old Man.

Blessed be!
Thank you!

When the First Door Opened

Suddenly he realized
that it had been nearly 38 years
since he had run away to break free.
Leaving as often as he came in the early times,
he remembered shying away in the night
unbeknownst to anyone who might care.
"Go pan for gold," his mind had enthused.
"Do something exciting or die!"
He remembered back to a hot, muggy April Fool's Day of 1979
when he found himself giddy,
driving 1,000 miles from Houston Texas
to learn that there was six feet of snow
and a torrential river on Pike's Peak Colorado.
How, excitedly craving adventure, he had turned the car around,
not knowing if he were Miami or Phoenix,
just somewhere, anywhere else bound.

He still felt a twinge of shame that welled in his gut
for abandoning his car in Waco
when he had run out of gas and money
and had no car title on him
since he had been waiting for it in the mail.
He couldn't abide the thought of waiting in Waco for it!
He left behind his teen's life's possessions and identity
and some pride
in that Wal-Mart parking lot.
He took three duffel bags stuffed full to lug down the road.

Still vivid and haunting,
the first door that opened for him
was a scowling young buck of a cowboy
who picked him up.
They had only driven about 5 miles when he pulled off
onto an old dirt side road

and slammed to a stop.
He yanked out his erection,
grabbed the back of his new passenger's head,
forced his mouth down on him
and made him gag and cower against the door.
He remembered how he had thought about biting it off,
but didn't believe he would live if he did.
Then the cowboy kicked him out
¼ mile off the 2-lane country road.
At least he'd let him have his duffels.

The second door that opened for him
was a friendly mother and her daughter.
They fed him pot roast,
allowed him a shower, an overnight on the couch,
gave him sweets for his journey,
and a joint,
and drove him ½ an hour to the next good place to hitch.

The third, a handsome black trucker,
let him ride all the way to Phoenix.
He smiled thinking about having secretly craved
the same thing, only in a kinder offer,
that the first had tried to make him do.
But those things were too dangerous in his mind.

Never to be forgotten, the fourth door opened
on the East side of Phoenix
after he had slept among great over-hanging trees
in the 4 lane's median strip.
A young man promised a ride as far as New Orleans.
He thought the young man had seemed a nice man
and good conversation flew.
After three days of travel
this pleasant man offered him
an open door to a life back in Phoenix,
a place with him and his girlfriend,
and a possible job too.

WAITING ON THE MONSOONS FOR HIS DESERT SOUL · 143

So around he turned again to start anew.
Three days later, arriving in Tempe
the driver inquired if he wouldn't mind waiting at Denny's
while he went and talked to his girlfriend
about all that had transpired.
24 hours later he still sat at Denny's,
the driver never returning,
all his duffel bags lost
in the guy's back seat,
a pair of shorts, a t-shirt,
and tumbled road sneakers to his name.
The hopelessness and disbelief still palpable 38 years later.
He recalled sitting there for 24 hours
just watching and waiting.
He was sure there must have been some mistake or an accident.
The night waitress fed him coffee and potato fries,
gave him three dollars of her tip money,
and a baseball cap as he downtroddenly trudged
out into the 111 degree morning.

He had then trekked through the sweltering heat
until he met Earthquake Red.
The old young man let him sleep on three old tires stacked high
in his ramshackle camp,
told him to keep his feet off the desert floor to avoid scorpions.
Under that desert night sky
he thought, for the second time, that he might die out there.
The prophesier of earth's shakes
took pity on some poor kid
and gave him a slightly better pair
of worn-out tennis shoes
to get him on his way.

Brother Michael, a Jesuit,
drove him up to his cabin
at the White Mountain Apache reservation.
He gave him a good dinner,
a nice night's sleep in his own little bed,

and took him to a graduation ceremony
at the local school for native children,
then drove him another hour
to the main highway.
He still wondered if that priest were gay.
He felt some hidden feelings that had seemed to stir in the priest.
But he didn't want it to go any further.

It was still fresh that door number 7
dropped him in Albuquerque, New Mexico
where he slept in a back-breaking tree
outside a bright restaurant
where people chatted loudly in the parking lot
all night long.

Then number 8
picked him up from that lot
and drove his jeep south on I-25,
leaving him off on some dusty old ramp
in the middle of the desert,
in the middle of the day,
as he waited and waited and waited
for a single car to drive by.
The sky turned dark from the south,
and he watched
as a giant wall of sand bore down on him,
blackening the sky and his faith
and pelted him with bitterness.
As he jumped into a culvert
his only jar of water dropped and broke,
and he cowered against the onslaught.
He could cover everything except his low back.
By the time the storm abated,
a half hour later,
his low back was raw, and a foot of sand
wedged him up against the corrugated steel.

Brushing himself off, hungry like a thief,

WAITING ON THE MONSOONS FOR HIS DESERT SOUL

he started walking down the lonely, hot highway.
It was the third time that the thought
that he could die on this trek
niggled into his exhausted mind.

The delight of seeing that yellow jeep pulling over
still made him smile.
His 9th ride in his three weeks of journey
picked him up within 20 minutes,
drove him 20 miles,
and let him out in Socorro, New Mexico,
a place he later came to understand meant "mercy."
He used his last three dollars to
buy French fries and a plastic bottle of water.
He walked to the last ramp out of town,
ready to head once more to Miami,
but as he walked he heard a voice inside his head,
loud and demanding.
It was the first time he had ever heard this voice.
It said, "Turn around,
there's something here for you!"

As he turned and stood watching,
he saw a white van with amplifiers on top approach
and suddenly a voice came booming toward him,
"Hey, hey, hey, it's circus day!
Come see Nina, the 3,500 pound elephant.
See llamas, jugglers and clowns!
Two shows today at the rodeo grounds."

Then he remembered his amazement when the speaker
spoke right to him,
"Hey you, kid,
you want a job with the circus?
The sandstorm tore our tent up,
and we really need help.
You get paid everyday,
and you can leave whenever you want!"

And he thought back to that very moment
as he climbed into a truck to meet
"Road Runner Red, the Original Cowboy Juggler."
He knew his life had once more opened to a door
that would never let it be the same again.

Once a Clown

He became a circus clown
when he was a young and naïve man
not very sure if there was anything to laugh about.
In one of his first professional klutzy escapades,
he drove a pie tin full of whipped cream so hard
that his stage partner Spiffendifferus's real nose cracked and bled
all over the stark white cream
and across the stage dressing into a shame filled heart.

He had never wanted to be a clown.
It had never even crossed his mind.
The early clowns he'd seen usually either creeped him out
or were not very funny.
The horror flicks of bad clown dolls
come to life with a French chef's knife in tiny demonic hands
had not shown up yet,
but he still felt edgy at the sight of most clowns.
Marcell Marceau bored him to tears,
but the old clowny comics like Abbott and Costello,
Red Skelton, Danny Kaye, and the Three Stooges
had all taken turns as nursemaid balms to the ills of the world
thrown at a child of the 60's.

And circuses!
Well, they were just a quaint and tired thing of the past
that he didn't even think still existed.
But then came the freak sandstorm
that smothered him against a culvert with thought-grains of death
and then drove him to an oddly synchronous meeting
on a sparsely traveled New Mexican desert road.
And suddenly, at the run-for-your freedom-from-slavery age of 21,
he found himself helping a tattered old-fashioned tent show
that also had been pummeled by the same haboob.

He worked hard on that show,
carrying ship-worthy hemp rigging,
guying out ropes that anchored,
porting the back breaking wooden bleachers,
and tugging a monstrous tent canvass
that bent down on his body for $10 a day.
But he was not as able to put up the two-ring big top
as easily as the other roustabouts, and one day, after a few months
and some pulled shoulder muscles, the boss said to him,

"You are not really a roustabout,
so tomorrow you will go two weeks ahead of the show.
At 7 am each morning
you will put on your own clown makeup
and go out and promote my circus."

So he found himself
roaming streets of tiny western towns,
handing out free tickets to the "One Day Only" show.
And once again there he was, traveling lonely highways,
but this time he slept in his car, cleaned up at gas stations,
and tried to put clown makeup over splotchy face bristles
poorly shaved in cold water by early dawn light.
He became polyester acrid sweaty and dirt lot testy,
working 16 hour days for 6 days a week.
He hung the posters of the coming folk phantasmagoria
on phone poles, vacant store fronts, and in sponsor's windows.
He handed out thousands of free kid's tickets in the host town
and other small towns within 30 miles in any direction in one day.
He bought ads and did radio and newspaper interviews,
and he waved at anyone who was near to him.
He waved so much his whole body jackhammered up and down.
He waved pretending annoyance at anyone who avoided his eyes.
He honked the bicycle horn tied under his armpit.
He even stalked people down the street,
arms flailing like a lunatic,
to get them to smile or at least acknowledge,
or at the very least to get others to laugh.

And then, when handing a free ticket to get into the circus
to some awe faced child,
or a free family pass to some poor family,
the smiles he was gifted seemed to stoke an ancient fire within.

But he often ran into children who were caught up suddenly
by someone painted with a firecracker red, platypus smile
and who had white saucer doe-eyes flicked by looming giraffe lashes,
the sight of which stopped them dead in their tracks.
If they didn't smile immediately,
they would often burst into agonizing, cringe producing,
dread and terror filled screams
and were quickly hustled away by caregivers.

But some kids still stood in horror-tinged stillness
as they took in the sight of him.
They would half smile and half grimace
at all the bright country-club golfer polyester
that he wore from head to toe.
They would stare at the large baseball cap he sported
bobbing around with stitched-on, foot wide,
canary yellow plush deer antlers on each side
and then at his humungous orange with blue polka dotted tie
as wide as a pants leg and hung down to his knees
and then at the brash red, white, and blue striped slick suit coat
straight from the 1980 Republican convention
that billowed over his red, pink, and blue
striped faded bell bottoms,
on down to his oversized stuffed red Keds
and then quickly back up to his face.

Some might break into a smile, but many,
their lower lips quivering like they just weren't sure
whether to laugh or to cry
or to run or to cower under mom's skirts, just stared,
big eyes watching for any sign of danger or assurance.

But it was when he would stick out his hand to offer a handshake

that the waiting time ended.
The moment of truth would come.
He would air shake his hand up and down
when he mimed that their response might be yes
in an attempt at encouragement and friendliness.
His great plush yellow antlers would vigorously bob up and down.
Then he would swing his head side to side,
his antlers clearing stupid things off shelves that were unattached
when he mimed that their response might be no.
It was at that point of cosmic catharsis
that many children and a few straight men
ran screaming for their mommies.
Whole stores emptied,
and babies screamed curdled milk and blood,
and so many mothers and store managers beamed hate filled eyes
that he wondered what had scared these children?
And he worried that if he scared these children
then his days were surely numbered
in some kind of oggly-gaggly fashion
toward how long he could put up
with the unintended consequences
from frightening those he was supposed to entertain.
But the road giveth and the road taketh away.
After 4 different car engines had blown up with him
at the wheel in just 2 years,
the drunks that crashed into his fifth clown car and totaled it
didn't leave any clowns wanting to scramble out of it anymore.
He hung up his antlers and his polyester
and never used them again—
except one year to go to a Make America Great Again Rally,
but that's another story.

The Show Must Go On! But Wait!

There was the day,
after wandering in the desert for several weeks,
after being robbed of everything he owned,
after cowering in a culvert against a nearly smothering sandstorm,
after waiting in the blazing sun for hours without water,
that the circus van appeared out of nowhere
and over loudspeakers invited him along
to join the sand shredded small tent entourage.

There was the day early on
when baby Nina, the 3,500 pound elephant,
took the shot of whiskey,
glass and all,
and swallowed it.
They waited for the glass to pass,
not knowing if it might splinter and kill her.
They had to wait all night long and far into the morning.

There was the day
that Larry the cantankerous llama got Captain Bill, his trainer,
down on the ground,
and Captain Bill struggled to keep those mean feet
from stomping and cleaving him to death,
using all his strength to hold Larry up and away from him.
Larry's vile putrid sputum coursed across Captain Bill's face
into his gagging mouth
and his sight squelched eyes
until finally somebody heard and came to his rescue:

the day that Lucy,
the 4 feet long, male-hating blue macaw
climbed up Uncle Ralphie the Clown's leg
and sat on his shoulder.
She would just as soon bite off a finger

or a nose if someone she didn't like got too close,
but there she was sitting on *his* shoulder,
Uncle Ralphie, the electrified, live wire clown
had to silently, and unspastically, breathe
while she was coaxed down with a juicy slice of mango:

then the day
Uncle Ralphie was coaxed into taking Lucy, the man-hating macaw,
to entertain the children at the Orange Colosseum.
She leaped over the seat just as they started the journey
to land with one foot stuck in the front seatbelt,
at which point she began beating her mighty wings
and squawking like a maniac.
As she flailed and tried to bite him,
he stopped the car in the middle of the intersection
and jumped out,
only to realize that cars had stopped in all directions.
They were all looking with disbelief
as the psychedelically colored and textured clown
with big stuffed moose antlers bobbing off his hat
grabbed a stick from the back seat
and somehow loosed the foot of the brazen, blustering macaw.
Then he tossed some peanuts into the back seat
to which the panicked bird leaped for comfort.
Mouths were agape as he then jumped back into the front seat
to drive off with astonished eyes googling.
He couldn't wait to deliver her back home that day
and was never willing to take her again.

Then the day came
when the tent crew boss's daughter
got hit on the head by her father's sledgehammer as he set a stake,
and the days counted until she was not needing to be watched,
able to swing again on the slack wire.

And then the day happened
when Ed the new Head Ring Master
invited Peewee the Roustabout to ride along in his deluxe RV

to help him on the night drive
to "read the signs,"
and Peewee couldn't wait
to run away from the new Head Ring Master of Ceremonies
who tried to make him do things to him
as one of the "signs to read."
Then there were more endless days when
Cowboy huffed from the semi's diesel tank
and exposed himself on the hill,
and Baby Nina broke the three taunting drunk Mexican's arms
with one swipe of her mighty trunk,
and Spiff, Huckleberry, and Uncle Ralphie
were taken to the Carson City Police Station
under suspicion of trying to lure a young girl into their clown car
as they did advance publicity for the coming circus.

Then came the day
when his fifth and final clown car in just two years time
was rear ended and totaled by drunks.
Uncle Ralphie found himself waiting again
as Huckleberry the Clown
lay unconscious on the highway.
He waited for the ambulance and police to come.
And then, soon afterward,
he waited alongside another road,
leaving as he had come,
thumb in the air,
waiting for the next ride
and chapter of his crazy life.

Whale Songs

He couldn't recall
the song with which the old tent crew boss marked the rhythmic flow
    of time:
perhaps an old seaman's chanty,
mushed through the mouth of stained scrimshaw teeth
still clutching a half smoked unlit Cuban stogie off one corner.
The gruff bass voice
creaked out from his hulking vessel timbers,
connecting new tissue to ancient sound.
Especially clear, it rang the brash "clank" of his shiny gray sledge
as it walloped the wide head of the 3 feet long steel spike.
It had become indelibly etched in him
when the man 3 times as old as any man helping him
began to sing the stakes into the earth.
With his resounding cadence the old salt
impelled the sledges of all six men in the chaining gang
to deliver a loud, telling blow,
each in perfect clockwise succession,
to the stake in the center between them all.
He would continue the chant as long as it took them
to drive it in until only 6 inches outcropped.
Then, like a shimmering human octopus,
the six would move on to the next stake
and the next
and the next,
setting pylons deep
to the beat of his crew boss gathering-way song.

They moved enchanted, like one soul,
until all 120 stakes had been driven into the hard-caked earth
as the circus tent was soundly anchored in its new harbor.
The driving duet with the old man's eerie melody
against the haunting chorus of clank, clank, clank,
still bewitched him like whale songs connecting across oceans.

The memory of the elemental bonding of these six men
always returned him to that timeless sea.
Their great flukes of long hammers
stretched out from thick arms,
arcing out and up and over their bodies,
then swelling like a great breath taken
and driven downward to slap the surface.
It took him back to seeing Humpback mothers
teaching their babies to slap tails
against the waters.

He could still hear that clank, clank, clank and surreal song.
It always woke the town to the odd newcomers
who had mysteriously appeared to this out-of-the-way place
in its mundane routine of just everyday surviving.
The out of the ordinary sound
announced that the big top show of dogs and ponies
had come with exotic animals, death defying acrobatics,
and clown escapades:
an odd sounding that came with other-world smells
of grease paint, cotton candy, and dancing bear scat.
It carried an entrancing invitation that said,

"Come share our dreams and adventures!"
and then the next day would be gone,
a phantom ship in the mind's harbor.

But more than any of these,
he still could see the sacred sweat
streaming off grimy, thick necks,
strapping shoulders, and dirty, bulging biceps
as they channeled their souls of whales,
saltwater rivulets cascading down
desert dirt-smeared faces locked in ancestral ritual.
Lunar rhythms and solar wills transcending self
as one song,
one heart,
one beat

echoing across fair lots and fields, tent crew boss calling,

"Wake up!
Leave your small ponds behind and jump into the ocean."

A Most Hate Filled Name

We were the bundle of sticks* thrown on as kindling post
to heighten the flame and burn witches to ghosts.
Stoned under rocks and burnished on fences,
"Faggot," the curse with which it often commenced.

Along so many paths, the cry broke his serenity,
stole his composure, pushed him to enmity.
He never knew why? He didn't dress to look gay.
He didn't swish or flounce or even say, "Hey."

But throughout his life he was often the guy
singled out by teen boys on testosterone highs.
Four or five in a car out of the blue driving by,
hanging out windows, cursing, "Die faggot die!"

From Pittsburgh to Portland, from Hawaii to Maine,
he always seemed faced with the blazing refrain.
As he walked peacefully along, minding his own game,
"We're comin' for you faggot!" ringing out with sharp aim.

Sometimes he felt terror, and he believed they'd come back.
He'd hide in the bushes or try to hide his tracks
by turning on side streets or jumping over fences.
He could never be sure; he didn't want to take chances.

For a time, though, he often would just give them the finger,
but violence to violence never felt like the right answer.
So a kiss blown their way was a response for a while,
a wave, and a shrug, and an impervious smile.

But a wrench to the stomach was always there,
and sometimes all he could do was just stare
and trust in his gut he'd know how to run
if the car turned around on that day with no sun.

That day never came, though at times it felt close,
And to this day he still holds that ghost:
that a simple loving man, who happens to be queer,
will still be that kindling and no witch need be near.

Note: *It is stated that many of the witch burnings of the 1400- 1700's used gay men as the first to be set aflame before the fire reached the witch at the top. Hence the title "faggot," which means a kindling stick or bundle.

This is not just my story. This version of my story is mild compared to what others have gone through and continue to undergo. I have had my head pounded against a table, as well as suffered countless anonymous gut punches while in high school and walking on various busy city sidewalks when I was in my 20's. I hid out of a fear of death when I was young. I and my partner continue to be taunted at times now. A few years ago we even received a death threat. I am not that fearful anymore. The amount of freedom and acceptance we have gained in the last 40 years is amazing. Times are troubling again, and I fear a resurgence of venom. But I am out and proud and not willing to go back!! I do fear for the transgenders, and the other GLBTQ kids trying to just grow up right now. And if this helps even one person who knows me to change their attitude toward anyone in our community for the better, then it is worth sharing!

Among the Sacred Sun Drops

He remembered
his long ago marching along the barbed wirings
and live trapped paths of power and distinction,
pushing and pushed,
dedicated, yet angry, and lonely and forlorn.
Finding love
was really the biggest, sought-after degree.
He thought back to his earliest times,
feeling thrown off giddy-up laps,
then tugged away from protective apron strings
until idols became tormentors
and insecurities became oppressors.
Then it seemed no actual man would never betray him.
But he could always escape.
How cleansing beams of gold,
dappling through his thick woods hideaway
half a mile back on his father's farm land,
always welcomed him.

Like a secret lover
always freeing,
always allowing!
Hiding amid the delicate drops
of sunlight kisses in his wild place,
he could imagine phantom men dancing with him,
twirling and spinning in swirls of soft satin gauze,
rainbow sparks glinting from their sinuous friction,
igniting something he dared not admit aloud then
under many different palls of penalties.

His dreaming woods gave him hope
as he danced his covert sanity.
His life seemed always the challenge—
to even just be around men, let alone work with them,

a challenge to share anything beyond facts
with men who challenged everything,
to play sports with men who he could rarely be equal to,
and often seemed mocked by,
and the pain of falling in love with men
while, at the same time, becoming more and more sure
that they were all just mean-headed jerks.

He had run from them,
dared not say anything to them,
feared the lash from tongues of inquisition,
the scorn of male dynasties questioned,
the betrayals from those thought caring,
lying in wait with their own bitter self-hatred
for others who could be different.

He found some peace finally at 30
after he had dropped trying to become
what straight men wanted him to be.
He strode off toward his own chosen horizons,
began to live an openly gay life among supportive peoples,
including the first men he could see
as balanced, caring, daring to be authentic.
He thought back to when, at 35,
he had heard fellow gay men talking about their own
"heterophobia,"
and he realized that he had been, and still was,
afraid of the maleness:
the same judgmental unforgiveness in him
that he thought was maleness,
the same prideful righteousness.
And his heart opened to the detested man inside himself,
and he set off,
away from the safe gay communities
he had grown stronger in
and out into the dreaded world of the feared straight and narrow.
But the golden reflections of his old forest home
always followed him in his heart.

WAITING ON THE MONSOONS FOR HIS DESERT SOUL

And though many, many lovers came and went
through the years,
in his looking for love in all the hard places,
that sanctuary always called him home.
When in doubt and confusion,
he could always dance in his mind in his comforting wood.
Over the decades,
as more lovers came and went,
and new friends came without a gay bent,
and more people seemed better adjusted
than his scared little self could ever have imagined,
he still found many who had the old fears in their souls.
But many also came who had the nurturing growth in their hearts,
and he found that many men could be the protective balm,
the comforting haven,
the inspirited breath of life and beauty
blown into the original nostril of being
for each other.

And he welcomed the poetry of men,
and the men who could make poetry,
and he found both straight and gay men
who were at ease sharing their own sacred sanctuaries
where they could all dance with joy
among sacred sun drops of love.

Sanctuary

And again he found himself there.
Once more in the so-called "sanctuary":
once more in the "faerie refuge"
where he could feel driven crazy mad,
easily satisfied, and sometimes even amazed:
once more to dive into what he judged
as a dark-night-of-the-soul, two-spirit shamanic training ground,
which often seemed only to minister
to misfit, helpless fools and braying jackass man-children,
and where the three fingers, often pointing back at him,
confused him as much as the one finger he aimed.

And he found himself there at his beloved woodyard,
at his sanctuary within sanctuary,
stumbling through the east gate of new beginnings
with some perceived insult
mucking about in his soul.
He didn't stop to call in the directions,
the anger in his head brewing.
He didn't take care to thank the tree people,
the hatred in his heart stewing.
He raised his battle-confused axe high
and swung a head choppers' parlay.
The gnarly wheel of wood spat a big chunk of herself
to ricochet off his ankle.
He hopped and cursed a seaman's shag.
His second fling flung a flustered flip,
and the thick limb mama torqued about
to toss a left knee lurch and fumble.
His brazen mind spun out.
His rage plumed like Brutus the cocky rooster,
and his snarling face seeped a scurrilous steam
just as his unfocused severance hit the squirrelly juniper knot.
He watched in slow motion

WAITING ON THE MONSOONS FOR HIS DESERT SOUL · 163

as a fist of wood back-stroked off with a ferocious roar
and landed with a gut-wrenching crack
to smack the finally present fool's noggin'.
It knocked him to the ground,
his axe winging off behind,
a giant swollen goose egg erupting on his forehead.
Only then could he remind himself
as he lay on the ground nauseous,
clutching his star-studded universe of pain,
"I must enter this place with more respect."

The next day (after a headache of a night)
he returned to the east gate.
This time he chanted his mantras though his hoarse voice
and his prayers for wisdom and peace to the east.
He circled to each of the other directions,
throbbing head and glittering eye reminding him,
inviting the highest good for all.
Then he chopped,
and he sorted,
and he stacked,
and he breathed a breath as deep as the ocean.
And the chop went deeper
and hewed him to the bone of his soul.
He felt his body piston hot;
spirit lava coursed through his being.
He stripped to a t-shirt in the 30-degree weather,
his sinuses clear,
his heart pulsing strong,
his aim getting truer with each honest swing.

Then he realized
that his mind had stopped chattering.
His angst had subsided.
His fear was gone.

He paused to take in the sacred silence
and looked out over the amazing vista of green mountains,

the striated red rock and sandstone monuments.
The dogs whirled and played.
Five ravens wheeled about the sky,
and he realized that he felt vital,
a part of the breath of the land,
kin to the strength of the wood.
He became more aware of how *he* broke apart
and heated up
and surrendered.
And he recognized that he was at peace
and that sanctuary was always up to him.

For the People

(1)

One year he was invited to the Lakota Sundance
to dance as a "Winkte'."
That first day
the elder medicine man in charge of the ceremony
avowed to them,
their long skirts billowing out behind
toward the harnessed buffalo skulls
which still reeked where some old flesh still clung,
"You are Winkte'!
You are holy people!
You dance with both sacred triangles inside of you,
one on top of the other.
One spins clockwise
while the other spins counterclockwise."

The Sacred Fire keeper drummed
out past the west gate of the sacred circle
and sang a soft smudging song
by the blazing just-past-dawn fire.
Soothing juniper essence saturated the breeze.
The elder continued,
"In this dance you can do whatever you need to do,
and go wherever you need to go,
if you feel called to do it in the name of healing.
You are asked to assist in those places forbidden to others,
like the moon lodge is for most men.
You have special duties that only Winkte's can do
in order for this Sundance to happen correctly.
And you may even enter the east gate
if spirit calls you to be there."

The 5 men all turned to look past the sacred cottonwood,

festooned with tens of thousands of brightly colored prayer ties,
to view where only the Winkte's, if divinely called, might go.
The east gate was where Ever-Changing-Mystery
entered the ceremony,
and no person was ever supposed to be.

He felt an intense humility and responsibility flare within.
The medicine man added,
"What you are called to do in the name of healing
no one can question.
Not me,
not even the Heyoka, though they will try.
The mostly white faery Walk-Betweens' eyes darted back and forth.
Fear passed between them like lightning bolts
at the mention of the mysterious, feared Thunder Clowns.
"Have a good dance,
a ho metakuye oyasin," he finished, shaking each of their hands heartily.

(2)

That year he danced mostly along the side,
under the sponsor's canopy.
Very timid to the new experience,
he carried a single small feather and moved in tiny steps
until "Chief Shellbone" appeared on the third day.

The mesmerizing man's presence was seemingly felt by all,
pitch black leather chaps over the top of black pants
that stood out like no other dancer's attire.
His bare, shiny chest cascaded down
to a wide-roving, overhanging belly.
His thick silver mane hung down his back
held back by a medicine shield
with two long black feathers twisting in the wind behind.
Large, blackhole-eyes,
seemingly void of anything,
bore out from the chiseled Ute face.
They threatened to suck all life into them

if one dared to look.
He brandished a long black bull whip in his hand—
even more of an excuse to not even dare a glance.

Chief Shellbone "corrected"
the hapless, unwitting white Winkte'
several times that afternoon on "Lakota etiquette."
He chased him out from under the canopy
with a crack of his whip inches from his butt.
He chased him into the arena, loudly cackling,
his voice crisp like a crack of thunder,
"Winkte',
if you're gonna dance,
then dance!"
Another loud crack as the whip came down again
within a hair of his backside.

All the while several men "hung"
by buffalo bone thongs poked through their pectoral muscles
on long tethers strung to the living tree.
60 more men and women danced, mesmerized
in the sweltering heat,
and 100 more watched as sponsors
from the sheltered outer circle,
as the wild-eyed Heyoka hied
on the heels of the poor, startled Winkte'.
Out at the heart of the ritual,
the medicine man used a scalpel
to cut into a prone dancer's chest
as he lay on a great buffalo skin robe.
Other leaders swung their eagle wing fans
and blew their shrill eagle bone whistles.
Suddenly some of the crowd erupted
in great gaffaws of laughter
when the wild Ute Heyoka swaggered
after his now high-tailed prey.
His sparking voice resounding over the crowd,
"I'm gonna steal you off to Montana

and make you my wife,"
adding, "You're gonna fix me a fine supper
and bead me some beautiful clothes
when I get you home!"

But the roaring approval of the crowd
emboldened the once naïve Pennsylvania farm boy,
and he took off galloping like a giddy schoolgirl,
his skirt trailing in the wind.
A high leap in the air,
and a queer twittering giggle erupted from him
every time a whip crack landed near his butt.
Some eyes flowed with amused tears,
except maybe for the Winkte's,
which had a certain wide-eyed horror
blended with an exhilarated, altered world reality
mixed with an ancient spiritual certainty.

At the end of that dance
the Heyoka came up to him
and handed him a turkey vulture wing.
He told him that he himself had once danced with it.
They looked into each other's eyes as the shimmering man said,
"You test me Winkte'!
But I like it!
And I like what you do for the people!"

(3)

For 7 more Sundances,
where Heyokas bayed at his heals, he danced.
Where traditionalists questioned his place
and even threatened to pierce his butt and hang him to the tree,
he danced.
And where the dancers continued to thank him
for his courage and support of them,
he danced.
Chief Shellbone's gift of the turkey vulture wing in his hand,

the seemingly out of place white Winkte'
never stopped dancing hard for the people.

Two Spirit Dancing

(1)

He prays,
the healing wing of the turkey vulture resting solidly
in the grasp of his right hand,
its hilt swaddled in sweat stained, crimson cloth,
a strong psychic compliment
to its blue blackness.
He admires its glimmering sensuality
in the enrapture of a scorching high noon blaze of the sun,
the dark seemingly ecstatic
at its turn to shine, and the light,
welcoming home in its enfoldment.

(2)

He witnesses
the grandfather medicine man deftly slide a scalpel
under the thick mounded pectoral skin
held between his left hand's thumb and index,
and then, swiftly and delicately,
maneuver one pointed end
of the thick-like-a-finger carved buffalo bone peg
up to meet the sharp of the stiletto's face.
Dancing nose to nose,
the blade exits from under the now softly bleeding flesh
as the white finger of bone slips under the skin to take its place.
He internally grimaces
while leaning down to tap
the sole of the man's foot with his cleansing wing
to help release whatever might be ready to be let go.

(3)

He breathes the heady, earth-sweet smoke
of juniper needles and twigs.
Lit on the embers of the sacred fire,
they waft from the many smudge pots.
The spirit smoke
dances like ancestors through the circle.
Somehow it cools him and the others in their heat.

(4)

He feels captivated
by the almost insulting acridity of buffalo skulls
waiting to do their part in the ceremony,
mostly bone clean,
yet still with small clumps of flesh and hair rotting away.
He sweeps his fan atop each skull, 7 in total,
harnessed in a line at the opening of the west gate,
their faces turned toward the door of death and remembrance.
He thanks them for their sacrifice.
They will be yoked to the back of a male dancer,
again hooked to buffalo pegs slid and hooked under muscle
squeezed up between shoulder blade and spine.
Then the whole train of heads will be tugged
around the hem of the hoop of sacred ritual by the man
in a magnificent promenade of power calling.
He feels sorry for them, but honors their duty.

(5)

He blesses
the women and men committed to this vision quest.
He watches them lift achy, leaden legs, entrancing
to spirit chants rising
from the singers and drummers in prayer to the creator.
They bob mesmerizingly in place
on the outer edge of this circle,

gazing through eyes which speak of timelessness:
some transfixed in solemn prayer,
some lofted skyward in heartfelt atonement,
some vacated to faraway lands,
and some just bearing witness
to their body's attempt to maintain
this pace, this fast, this dance
through an exacting and exalting heat which withers and scolds,
yet also buoys the shimmering auric ethers of their souls.

(6)

He imbibes the exhilarating spirit essence
of determination, pain, and grief,
as well as that of joy and surrender,
spilling out of the hanging dancers' craned supplications
over now dry sweat and tear streaked arroyos
etched on wind and sun-seared countenances.

(7)

He dances, his feet touching the earth mother
in the northeast of the great Sundance wheel
while his spirit soars aloft
where his peace eagle wing tells him it is home.
He can almost inhabit him.
He senses him as a young male vulture
still exuding tremendous strength
and stamina
and will.
They move as one into a clockwise spiral.
He feels this awareness
soaring in the pristine, azure sky,
the sun warming his body,
the winds lifting it heavenward.
He asks his medicine partner to do in death
as he had in life:
to clean up the gore,

to eat away the dead,
to wipe the war field clean.
And he humbly beseeches him to help,
for he knows that he too is charged,
destined perhaps to clean up the energy
of that which is dying and dead
and no longer serves.
So, with wing in hand
the Winkte' warrior, follows
his young soul friend's lead.
And he soars into the sacred spiral
of ever changing mystery.

White Winkte' Day

(1)

The ceremony hadn't even really started yet.
Most celebrants had just gone out to fetch
the honored tree of life,
the cottonwood,
that they would loft high and portage back
to merge with the sacred earth mother.
There the vision seekers would fast, dance, and pray
centered around this emblem of fertility and promise
for four solid days.

At different times throughout the 4 days
different men would stand and lean backward from the sacred tree,
the bunched-up skin of their pectorals
tethered to it by a long rope.
They would try to coax the knot of skin above each breast to break,
 to release the buffalo peg that held the line,
waiting for a vision that would help them,
or their family or their community or the world.
Many would jerk, trying to break free;
some run and leap, looking for liberation;
most would pray and/or plead for their skin to break
so their prayer would be released from their body
and taken to *Tanka Shila* to be answered.
The women stood at different times of the ceremony
with pierced upper arm skin tethered to eagle feathers
and waited for the feathers to be yanked free,
for their vision to come.
Their need for suffering was much less compared to men, he was
    told.
After all, they had suffered through childbirth, he was told.

He was told that the Sun Dance

was started a hundred or more years ago
for the cleansing and healing of men
and that women and white Winkte's
were only recently allowed to participate.

He felt honored to be serving as a Winkte', white or not.

(2)

But he could not make himself go to get the sacred cottonwood tree.
A torment in his soul brewed, and he found himself mostly alone
with just a few fire tenders left behind.
He had just had an intense encounter with two young Lakota boys
whom he somehow knew
were being sexually abused in their everyday lives,
and it shook him up.

As he walked toward the sacred place
at the medicine wheel's center
where the tree would become the Sun Dance pole,
he felt overtaken.
He scampered down through the gaping maw of earth
that awaited the shaft's penetration,
his racing-mind-hold leading him heedless.
His bounding, edgy footholds
abraded his hidden-from-public scars.
He nearly leaped into the sacred gash
which was nearly twice as deep as his body was long
and only twice as wide
as his torso's claustrophobic breadth
as he found the bottom.

(3)

In the cool, dark womb he stood.
He breathed the ancestral, familiar, heady aroma of time
and slipped into the core of his own secret earth.
Suddenly the memory grabbed him again.

The soul-scared doe eyes
of the two chestnut brown Lakota boys
that had seared into his wiring earlier morning
and stared at him with psychic pleading.
They were eyes that cauterized something
in his own neuronic history.
Beautiful bright eyes that called him, with horror, to realize
that under their playful exteriors
they hid that they were being abused sexually.
He knew it with a certainty that sickened him.

Inside of him
the familiar essence of the sabre toothed tiger totem
he wore around his neck,
suddenly began to hiss and spat.
He felt her take up equal space within him
like he never felt her before,
soul bone deep and true,
somehow sharing a space of consciousness together with him.

(4)

Suddenly, he and the old cat
began to wildly claw at the packed clump matrix.
He sensed her great paws sweeping
in an ancient, mother-fevered raking.
His own soft healer's hands tore at roots,
shredded shard-sharp dried clumps,
bruised bone on stubborn blockade.

They bore their bleeding hearts
through scratched, raw skin and psyche.
It trembled them
like some long festering cosmic wound
that had begun to burst and pour forth seeking redemption.

The thought of the two boys being abused tore at him,
and great snarls emerged in his ferocity.

The cat and his rage and confusion and grief merged.
His mouth screamed as the cat's rasp-growl bellowed.

Torrents of tears and mucus filled their mouths.
It splat from their blustering, angry heads,
mixed with sweat runneling down their face
and pooled with the dry world skin breaking.

The quickening congealed an ancient angst,
married the depth of shame root and bitter bone,
and ran bound by kindred blood that boiled rage
to release the buried echo.

(5)

In a final stillness he knelt
spent at the bottom of the sacred honoring.

He sourced through the eyes of the ancestral mama tiger
who could bear to see no children suffer.
He felt the two Lakota boys beside them,
teary and slightly smiling.
The light of day was now directly on him,
blazing against the crown of his head.

He sensed the old medicine man in the hole with him,
and he was called to remember all the tales
he'd heard about the vanquished tribe,
including many of this dance's leaders:
boys once sent away to Christian boarding schools,
some raped by their white male teachers,
psychic scars still hidden,
and he felt them in the hole with him and the cat,
and all the men and boys
that had ever been raped by oppressive men
in the whole of time
seemed in that hole with him and the cat.

And he felt uplifted to think that maybe
the truth would be able to now emerge,
that maybe even understanding and forgiveness
could heal the oldest human wounds.

(6)

When he finally crawled out into the new birth of his day,
he found himself facing a giant buffalo
shimmering like silver curtains.
It was an etheric creature standing immensely tall
and towering over him
just inside the west gate, a few feet from him.
Its giant head seemed to be mere inches from him.
He could feel its great swath of breath blow on him,
could hear, and even feel, a heavy hoof paw once at the ground.

He felt tiny in the shadow of the surreal mammoth.
But the buffalo looked down at him
and thanked him with tears in its eyes.
He met the tears with his own humble ones.

Such was the beginning of another year
where men too could open to heal their ancient scars.
He wondered if he should tell
the Lakota medicine man about this,

or let it be just another white Winkte' day.

The Potter

(1)

He looked at himself
in the clay clasped in his prayerful hands.
He remembered when he was too green,
unformed, and unrefined
to know about the ways of pottery
and the ways of love.
He had tried to hold on so tight
to so many delicately forming embodiments.
It took a long drying time in himself
to realize that his shaping tools were often blunt and indelicate
and his pressure too ponderous and needing to push and clutch.
He felt the resignation in himself about his clumsy handlings
that had destroyed so many miraculous creations,
and he still felt grief at the long line of loves lying broken
like smashed pueblo pots tossed off cliff-side homes
to avoid contamination and death.
He lamented that no amount of slip
had ever made him able to touch and hold,
or be touched and held,
with any kind of lasting integrity.
He felt resigned that his slip,
for much of his life,
was almost always very conditional— at least until he met Rose.

(2)

He felt himself
in the soupy red clay squishing between his fingers.
In its ooze he squirmed to recall
the slippery lusts that often had come to melt time
and focus
and compassion.

The thick clay clots in the goop
merged into the abandoned guilt
that had early on bound him up
when he had had no patience
for the delicate unfoldment of other spirits into their flesh.
This all led him to his own drenching shames
when his waters, wanting their immediate gratifications,
kept deluging his foundations,
softened them to crumble,
and everything just glopped into hideous distortions of dreams.
He remembered that there was nothing seemingly formable
into anything with strength or character or stamina.
How many times he had had to start anew from this!
He sighed, thinking of how often
he had wistfully rolled out the next slab of his life's clay,
moving from job to job, lover to lover, place to place.

(3)

He looked back at his life of clay.
He remembered
that as a young vessel in scorching kilns
his passions had blazed,
and his colors had often burst forth
with pride and invincibility.
That was often followed
by shattering eruptions
that blew his walls of so-called "reality"
into sharp, dangerous shards of fractured trust,
bleeding out from his own broken shell.
He remembered as well
the many heart-cold kilns
where his apathy reigned,
and all was drab
and inevitably abandoned
until the drive to create again
pushed him back into centering.
He felt he had been thrown on the wheel so many times,

and he was glad the spinning had finally gotten mostly even.

(4)

He thought about a pottery mentor who once said,
"Throw 100 cups and then smash each one
to get the sense of its,
as well as their,
overall character.
And he wondered,
and he came to believe
that his own first hundred cups had probably mostly been smashed.
He prayed that his cracks must bare witness
to some kind of honorable depth and strength
as well as a whole lot of grace
from some other forming hand.

Just a Tiny Teacup

(1)

I was just a tiny teacup.
The ocean poured into me.
I tried to hold its power for just an instant,
but I overflowed to weep.
No sounding line able to fathom,
we sailed in an ancient stew of civilization.
We sensed the roll of times and tides
rising and falling like the 20 feet tall walls of waves
that thrust life and death rhythms against the prow
of our strong, yet frail, colossal floating city:
12,000 years of empires of history at the broths' edge,
built one atop another atop another:
man's mountains ever replacing gods,
yet all tumbling back to the sea.
Like a cast from a Fellini flick,
we eight intrepid explorers
followed a rare sojourn of an eternal path.
Our sea legs wobbled
as we roamed like Dionysian revelers,
cavorting gaily down narrow city corridors.

We stared slack-jawed at Ruebens, Rembrandts, Picassos,
swelled at Caravaggios,
astonished at meticulous Michelangelos,
and marveled at gaudy Gaudets.
We stood humbled by the still-looming dinosaur bones
of colossal temples to Zeus, Athena Nike, Apollo
that called all to look up to their gods.
We stuck our fingers in wooden wheel ruts
on gleaming marble streets that charioteers drove upon,
that Antony and Cleopatra strode upon,
that gladiators pushed slaves along to coliseums

for the blood sport entertainment of the day.

We feasted in awe and disgust
at the popes and their fortunes:
the towering cathedrals,
myriad tombs of saints and martyrs,
gilded frescoed chapels,
and luxurious tapestries depicting biblical proportions.
Coal black pharaoh mummies lay encased behind glass
amid the triumphant display of the voluminous treasure
of conquered "heathens" and "inferior gods."
We strolled vast chambers, their stained-glass portals
inviting glorious Mediterranean skies to blaze through
(except in this record breaking cold and wet winter)
to behold Christianity's pride and privilege (and perversion).

(2)

Back on board,
mythical Circes chanted whispery siren songs from mystical isles
jutting up like the tips of Poseidon's trident,
slipping by in the black of Odysseus's somber nights.
They rekindled Scylla dreams of Turkish men's large, dark eyes
laughing, smiling, inviting,
exerting Trojan horse fears
under Istanbul's minarets, calling prayers to be answered.
Our green stomachs,
sated in orgiastic gastronomic overwhelm,
honored the gluttonous pride of the decadent Romans,
my direct fore-bearers.
We hastened to absorb,
to attempt to understand in the hectic scramble to witness
as many sights possible of one of history's cradles
in just 12 days at sea
and 8 hours at each of 6 country's ancient capitals.
The dark, foreboding skies drizzled cold, dampening rain
constantly.
The seas churned an eternal baptism of holy salt spray.

(3)

I remember,
as we drove the rich farmland of Italy on our way to Rome,
the beautiful farmhouses, their red adobe colored ceramic roof tops
nestled amid fig, olive, and cypress trees.
It brought back something genetic in my bones,
and my cup overflowed tears of cloudy remembrance.

I remember in Ephesus, Turkey,
at the place Mary, mother of Jesus,
lived her last few years and was buried,
that the garden birds called with delight.
The gushing spring that touched her lips still offered atoning waters.
In her house a soothing balm
comforted from the coldness of the outside world.
Here, too, I wept an ocean of unknown grace.

And yet again,
as our vessel approached the ancient foundation were Troy once
    stood,
a blood red sun-rising, shimmering of fire
squashed down upon the memorial
of the ancient city-state fortress that once stood impregnable.
I was reminded of the city of Cairo;
that, too, was burning blood red in people's revolution,
a one day journey beyond to the west.
Once more I wept as ghosts of empires past
reached out to the future ghosts of empires present,
making me feel smaller than any Parthenon on a shining marble hill.
Yet I was more trusting than any ocean surrounding me:
this tiny teacup flowing through the vapors of time.

Nature of Things

(1)

The gnarled hand of the tiny, stickly woman begged upward.
Her head, slumped over bones,
crumpled along the street's bank, waiting.
The mostly heedless stream of humanity flowed by,
nearly stepping on her to make headway,
bobbing along in their own torrents and eddies.

The little jungle village turned city thronged with a vibrant pulse.
The narrow sidewalks were awash
with a multitude of mostly small brown people.
Bright, primary-colored Honda rickshaws controlled all the thin
    streets
as they hauled tourists and laborers
and the citizenry about in their daily routines:
suitcases, live and dead chickens, lumber, great swags of bananas,
and other produce hanging all about them,
their thrumming engines buzzing like bees.
Their infesting sound, dying down to nothing as 40 to 50 of them
all seemed to come to the few downtown stop lights en masse
and then rev like hornets suddenly swarming
as the lights turned green.

A few blocks down
the throngs of humanity, with their desert-island eyes,
swept by another waif woman marooned onto the street's
    shoreline.
This one was blind, but with an almost beatific smile on her face
and a bliss that touched her with grace.
The peace of her journey seemed to hold trust
behind her sanctuary-eyes
as seemingly empty boats flowed past.
He, too, turned his head quickly away from her,

his heart choking in its own brine.

Iquitos, an ancient village of river trade,
was a rubber boom town in the 1940s.
Now it was filled with crumbling, old Spanish churches
and rundown buildings heaping upon each other.
This beautiful island city, surrounded by five rivers
converging as headwaters of the Amazon,
still showed the evidence of torrential flooding
from the last monsoon season three weeks earlier.
Impoverished people (by Western standards anyway)
still tried to deal with swept-everywhere trash and sewage
and thatched huts missing walls
and roofs torn open to show the few possessions that most had.
Pools of water and mud were everywhere
if you went anywhere off the few asphalt streets.
Fetid air sometimes lingered amid the jungle merged urbanity.
Ripening mildews flavored the air
among masses moving briskly in day to day bustle
While outside the city jaguars, anacondas, piranhas, javalinas,
as well as the human animals lurked:
the jungle guerillas that were fighting with them
as well as with the miners and de-foresters
and other robbers stealing from all their lands.
These all added to a host of elements that made life here
seem just too juicy for him.

(2)

But the people seemed so alive
and full of energy and vibrancy like the streets,
especially the people of the different local tribes.
Those who brought their handmade jewelry and clothes
and other commodities to sell everyday,
porting their goods on the rivers,
thronging for each tourist.
Dozens and dozens of them would appear,
hands outstretched, brimming with alligator paw necklaces,

jaguar pendants, macaw feather earrings, boar tusk emblems,
and a host of other things.
A barrage of begging would ensue,
"Look at my stuff. Look at my stuff.
I give you good deal!"
Dozens of them,
mostly young to teenage boys with their family's goods
who would sell the things and take the money home
to their families in the jungle,
would suddenly surround tourists,
especially white American ones.
He got the image of them once,
as if they were like the piranha he saw being fed on the Amazon,
carving up the water rabidly.
It was a hard image with which to blemish them,
and he sometimes had to stem the rise of inexplicable fear in himself.

But he had quelled that fear mostly,
buying a little each day from one or two of the young sellers.
Everyday he promised that he would look
at the others' wares the next day,
but everyday more young ones would come around.
Then his own poverty consciousness would growl within,
knowing the funds were going quickly.
He had mostly just the money needed to get home
and face some of his own survival issues,
but his heart had felt their need, and he could not stop himself.

On the last day of his journey
a very young one came to him and said,
"I show you my stuff now?"
and he looked at him with great sorrow and said,
"I have spent all my money.
I have nothing left to give."
The little boy, with tears in his eyes, said,
"But I'm hungry!"

Then he gave him the last two soles in his pocket.

3)

Years later, home in his comfort,
he still fights back tears remembering
the little boy's face and the desperation in his voice.
And he had to wonder,
what would The Donald* have done?
Then he cries a little more.

Note: *Donald Trump

Do You Sing In Your Cage?

Peace like a river flowed
in his last few days before execution.
17 years on death row,
the one whom mostly everyone,
even the guards on his block,
believed to have been falsely convicted of murder,
glowed in absolute tranquility.
He praised God in voice and song.
It is said that if you cage a hummingbird
it will lose its joy,
stop singing,
and die.
But he had sung everyday,
sometimes all day and all night,
through all the troubles and trials.
He had forgiven everybody.
There was no one he could find anything bad to say about.
A dear friend and his mother watched him walk
through the door to his demise
with utter peace, dignity glowing.
His mother said he had sung all his life.
The friend said she had felt her own trust reborn.

(2)

In a book by Holocaust survivors
about the "saints" in prison camps
who marched to their deaths with dignity and peace,
they said that those were the ones
who never let the cage bars shred their faith.
They were always singing,
outwardly in the balm of their calming ministrations,
inwardly when the smell of humans burning
could imprison their souls.

They said kindness and compassion
always shone on their countenances
and in their actions,
even towards their executioners.

(3)

To the ancient Mayans
the hummingbird was the warrior,
intensely fierce,
protective,
territorial,
and sacredly aggressive.
My father was a hummingbird,
although I often questioned
the "sacred" part in his aggression.
I remember my father,
throughout his life,
sang when he was happy,
which didn't seem very often.
But in his last days
the warrior sang loudly and constantly
to transcend
the intense physical pain.
His last words to his distant son,
"I can't die yet,
I've only just begun to do what I want to do."
I think he left this plane feeling betrayed
by his chosen cage
that held the promise of a later freedom.
I think he forgot to keep singing until it was too late.

(4)

Is the rash of people being slaughtered
being done by hummingbirds with out-of-sync-aggression?
Do they feel caged?
Have they lost all their joy?

Have they forgotten how to sing?
Maybe the biggest place we've gone wrong
is not helping little boys
remember the sacred in their own songs.

The Culling Times

(1)

"Happy New Year,"
he remembered muttering aloud into the brutality.
He could feel again his eyebrows arc in mockery.
It was 7 a.m.,
and the TV weather station had said it was -18 degrees outside.
"That was just yesterday,"
he thought back with disbelief at all that had transpired in 24 hours.
His fingers and toes reminded him
that yesterday morning they had been achingly stiff,
the arthritis cooperating like cranky, frozen bolts.
He grimaced, recalling how his heels and nose had burned with desire
for anyplace warm enough for some comfort—
to not be struggling in his thin framed home,
electric heaters taxed to a roaring growl,
eskimoed under 3 cotton blankets and 2 Pendleton's.
His bones had rattled like his skin was just cold tin and his organs
    stone.

(2)

He recalled how he had finally forced himself
out of the door yesterday
to set out for the outpost.
He knew a roaring stove, inches away, would help.
His psyche had clattered and chattered mockingly
as ice weevils gnawed at his fabric of tolerance and survival.
He still shivered, recalling the walk,
bundling himself to himself,
the promise of the sun
just peeping above the blocking mesa toward the East,
and he remembered hearing himself say,
"Many will choose to die this day."

(3)

He pieced together yesterday's timeline again:
how he had walked the few hundred feet like it was the Iditarod trail,
then stood nearly over the hooting, hissing pot-bellied stove at the outpost
that roared like a banshee's yearning:
how his burning toes had suddenly rekindled a memory
of his once-frozen 13-year old feet.
Stuck in poor hunting boots
in brutal Pennsylvanian deer hunting season,
both his feet and he had been trapped in an agonizing wait.
He again pulled up the old despair
of being left alone,
from long before the light could comfort,
in the thick brushed huckleberry swamp miles from his family's farm:
lost to direction,
told to not move,
everything aching, shivering,
dismal.
He still could feel his anger.
Resentment had smoldered hot and pitched,
even as he also recalled
the wild anticipation of deer maybe being herded toward him.
His icicle toes at the edge of the stove's reach
still lived in the memory
of the torturous hours interminably passed that morning long ago
when no deer came
and no father or brother or uncle emerged from the thicket
for hours and hours and hours.
He remembered his amazement at the terror
still sitting in his old man's body, remembering itself
as small and forgotten and abandoned,
helpless,
maybe freezing to death.
He again shook himself off to the fire.

(4)

He recalled mulling to himself,
after his feet were finally warm enough
to not throb on the walk back to his iced-over cave,
that throughout time torturous cold spells
had probably persuaded and propelled many
to leave their bodies behind forever.

Then the feral kitty had raced toward him,
yelling adamantly at him from behind.
She, that for months
had yelled every morning at him from under the porch,
but never allowed him to get closer than 5 feet,
had run in front of him.
She had plunked herself down between his heavy, booted feet,
stopping her movement,
scooting her butt upward at him,
inviting,
begging.

"My goodness," he remembered himself saying,
"It is quite a New Year's Day.
Wild beast tamed by the need for love."
He ran his full hand from butt to shaggy head several times,
the elevenish sun beaming intensely
against the blinding, raw, sugar-crystalized driveway.
The magnificent brush of charcoal puffball,
that had stopping declaiming at first touch,
was suddenly purring into long luxurious suppleness.
He smiled as he recalled her flopping onto her side,
welcoming several full ministrations,
and then how quickly she had jumped up then trotted ahead.
"Ready to take on the day again, huh?"
He sighed, thinking aloud,
"we all could use a little encouragement
to know that someone could care
on such a brutal day".

(5)

Then he remembered the end of that brutal day yesterday,
the smell of an electrical malfunction smoldering from the heater
    closet.
They had kept their breath and their wits,
calmly taking their most valuable possessions to a neighboring cabin,
shutting down their home
and trundling out into the remorseless equalizer.
He felt thankful once again that something had warned them early
so as not to be culled from the herd as they slept.

"Happy New Day!" His new refrain.

"Witch Hunt, the Real Thing"

She was condemned:
"That she did wickedly, maliciously, and feloniously covenant with the devil.
Did sign the devil's book with blood.
Did give herself soul and body to the devil.
By which wicked and diabolical covenant,
she is bound a detestable witch."
She was hanged along with Rev. George Burroughs.

(18 others were later hanged as witches. One was squashed by stones.)

Her sons, Andrew, Richard, and Thomas,
were imprisoned and tortured to weigh against her.
Her 7-year old daughter was forced to announce her as a witch in court.
Rev. Cotton Mather pronounced that she was "a rampant hag"
and promised her that she would be the "Queen of Hell."

It is told that she was plain and outspoken,
of remarkable strength of mind
with a keen sense of justice and a sharp tongue.

Her husband, the former Royal Executioner,
had chopped off the head of Charles the First.
Now Charles the Second really wanted to have his head.
Her husband had run to the colonies to escape the King's wrath.
She had met him, twenty years her senior, and married him.
They had moved to Andover because of her sharp tongue in another town.
Once there she continued on the same path.
She fought constantly with neighbors
whom she thought had cheated her husband in business affairs.
She mightily castigated impious behaviors.

She threatened God's vengeance on the many not as holy as her.

Of those many threatened,
a few suddenly developed swellings in their legs,
or their cows stopped giving milk.
One cow just died.
One man got a pain in his side, which
"Bred a sore that discharged several gallons of corruption."

Then she let her children go out and play with neighboring children
when they were in the last stages of smallpox.
The disease spread, and thirteen would die from it,
including her brothers and two nephews.

This threatened the stability of the community.
The "hexings" that she seemed to constantly discharge
were joined with this latest affront.
All of this was added to stories of children
who had seemingly been bewitched the year before up in Salem.
There, several girls had exhibited twitchings and convulsions
and told tales of witches flying on brooms in covenant,
of talking malevolent cats, and other hysteria.
The town of Andover brought two "Salem Victims" to identify any
    witches in Andover.
The process of scouring the community for witches called her as one
    of the first possibilities.

Her frenzy of a trial was similar to the ones in Salem.
The two afflicted Salem girls said they saw the thirteen ghosts of
    those
that she had murdered flying around her.

She called them liars.
Then she turned and scolded the magistrates
"For believing the specious assertions of hysterical children.
It is a shameful thing," she cried,
"that you should mind these folks that are out of their wits."

Suddenly the children panicked and issued "intolerable outcries and
    agonies."
Guards were summoned to haul her out in chains.
Neighbors and family came forward to denounce her as a witch.

Through it all she defied them.
She boldly bared her innocence.
She was the only one among the accused
who did not make an admission or confession.
On August 19th of 1692,
my 7th great grandmother, Martha Allen,
was loaded onto the back of a cart with four convicted men
and transported to Gallows Hill.
She was there hanged.
Her children were made to watch as a lesson.

It is written that she "died well,
neither overborn in mind nor shaken in nerve
and met death with heroic courage."

Know Your Bones

The agonizing clench in the middle of his spine gave him pause.
The x-ray diagnostics still tumbled through his mind.
New words in regard to his bones pulled him to reflection.

He thought about how his break-out-of-the-box bones
had carried him all over an amazing world,
how his color-outside-the-lines bones
had allowed him to try all kinds of things
in the pursuit of his authenticity
and the search for his heart's mission,
how his "leave-me-alone" bones
had thrown him to adventures that any writer would crave:
to lovers that taught him to love himself,
to *Kripalu* yoga bridging him back to original bone.

He thought about his father's bones:
how his strong bones toiled for most of his life
farming and family raising
and welding in an iron working factory;
how his Capricorn bones made him "productive,"
but over worked and sizzle-tongued
from the betrayals and bafflements
of things and people he deemed illogical,
which were most humans;
how he tried to hide his achy hearted bones
gotten from caretaking his ever more senile mother
who no longer recognized him
and was lost to land's unknown for her last 30 years;
and how the bones in the garden of his soul
seemed bitter about almost everything.

He recalled the day his mother called him,
worried about his father,
who was suddenly lethargic and weary.

His father soon afterward died quickly and unexpectedly
because his bones had quit producing white cells,
a condition called Leucopenia,
an apt metaphor for his "poverty of light."
His last words to his distant son on his deathbed,
"I can't die yet;
I've only just started to do what I've wanted to do."

He thought about his mother's bones,
bones that were a medical curiosity.
While most old bones grew brittle,
hers got thicker and stronger.
Scores of doctors studied her for over half her lifetime,
trying to discover how her bones,
once abandoned as a given-to-relatives "Depression "child,
grew encircling;
how her bones, as a "corn fed" girl, grew hefty to work hard;
how her bones as a mother of four beloved boys
stretched willingly to do whatever it took.
Her bones seemed to ache a quiet longing.
She married two physically strong and protective, but angry men.
But more than that, she held on to God,
and the bones of her existential skeleton
grew strong and robust
while the bones of her body
became one of six causes of her death.

People called her a saint.
She was a Taurian who toiled heavily,
yet seemed to arch her bones
with an ear toward the music of the universe
and a want to channel its beauty and kindness.

He looked back on how the path of his own bones,
acute spinal curves tweaking and poking his everyday
    consciousness,
had taken him on a twisting journey of ancestors and self- discovery.
At times his bones had weighed him down,

but he recognized that they also could make him feel alive.
He looked back at how they had made him courageous enough
to step beyond anticipated pain:
how they had made him humble so that he could finally ask for help,
how they had continued to open him to find more patience,
to listen to his intuition as old patterns could no longer be applied,
and to innovate outside his Virgoan strictures
and how they had helped him to finally grieve
and to pray.

His bones talked to him every day.
He wondered if he would fully know
the secrets of his bones before he died.
He was sure he had but to listen to them
as they clattered and schemed in the bone jar of his life.

The Hand Me Down Bullet (Or Man's Eternal Hernia)

From the hole in his loin's brain,
for the ancient father's insanity drain,
the forgotten raging-inside silently proclaimed,
"Never more will you hear me.
Never more will you know me.
Behind this wall I enclose me.
From me to you, I die!"

From the split in his seam
that spilt out squashed dreams,
the psychic castrati awakened shotgun shell memes.
40 years of swallowed conflagration
sputtered bullets of self-emasculation,
echoed, "You'll never be as good as me
at anything you try!"

From a tear in his universe
an echo screamed a muddling verse,
twisted, seeking for man's line curse.
"Where's your guts, eggshell walker?
Sittin' spittin' out storm cloud stalker.
Better get busy or I'll kick you in that lazy ass."

From a rip in the weave the cosmic muttered,
a dredged-up muck stuckly uttered,
caused his heart to flip and flutter.
"Here's your daddy, flop tit fatty.
I'll give you something to make you sad.
I beat you again;
you'll never last!"

From the gut wise hatch's re-lashing

WAITING ON THE MONSOONS FOR HIS DESERT SOUL · 203

came reflection of his courage dashing
in self-lockdown prison walls slowly smashing.
A thousand times it happened: if one
had a dream, a task, some fun,
a choice of guts the only gun
to just get out of bed to face a day.

From the reweaving of karmic shifts
cosmic limp dick ridiculousness began to lift,
a conscious choice to neither shoot nor self-inflict.
His life's reflection from gaping intestines:
"Where's your guts?" he had no question.
They came each moment
he had told another man he was gay.

Waiting on the Monsoons for His Desert Soul

He hated the way June bore into him
like the dratted no-see-ums
that tangled in his body hair
and bit deep gouges that festered and pocked.
Desperation coursed strong and hard through his ragged veins
blistered by the sun's scorch,
throttled by the choke of his parched prayers.
He thought with exasperation,
"The Zuni's MUST be doing their rain dance by now."

A young mountain lion had come down a few weeks earlier
when the oppressiveness had already seemed relentless.
It had easily leapt over the 5 feet tall perimeter fence
and snagged a couple of chickens roosting too low in the junipers.
He had to corral the rest of the girls
into the fortress solid chicken house after that,
so that the returning lion couldn't feast and would move along.
It had come back 5 nights in a row looking for an easy meal.

He prayed, "Drum hard, Zunis.
Call the thunder beings to appease all that hunger."

He got a few more young chickens to replace some of those lost.
Old man raven broke through their enclosure,
tore their heads off, and ripped hearts out of their breasts.
Sickened, he had raced 60 miles to the nearest town
to build a better enforced cage for another start.

He pleaded, "Dance hard, Zunis.
Call the water gods to quench all that thirst."

He answered, with resigned surrender,

his far away friends when they asked
if there was anything more that could be done.
"Just a few more weeks until the monsoons come.
Life is just this way here.
Everything goes on pretty normal until June
when the heat really starts to build
to bring rain to the continental divide again.
It has been so long,
but for now we must wait.

"We build stronger enclosures.
We pay closer attention.
We use only as much of the sacred scarce water
as necessary to keep things alive.

"We know the animals struggle.
The people struggle.
The plants struggle.

"We are called to learn to trust in the course of things
beyond our control.
We have to work to hear
and gentle the inner reactions of our nature
because we know we cannot control
the nature outside ourselves.
Such is June here."

He kept praying, "Sing hard, Zunis.
Call the grandmother rain to comfort all of us."

He watched the heat get to his turkey hen.
She kept going out onto the old county highway
where she dared cars to take her on.
Her big breast puffed out and her body flared.
One car apparently took her on.

Her free ranging partner, the guinea hen,
now just calls and calls and calls.

All day long the shrill squeak,
like a rusty hand pump to an old well,
drills into all ears and all nerves.

He feels his own exhaustion.
He pushes against the heaviness in his own
chest, the thirst of his own spirit,
the grating squeak of his own nerves.
He chews some osha to break up the dry clot.
He takes an afternoon nap
because there is nothing else he can do out in the inferno.
He sips a little more water.

He can't watch the news
because all that he sees are oblivious chickens, cocky turkeys,
desperate lions, and cruel ravens.

He gets out his hand drum
and beats an unknown, but familiar beat,
"Come on Zunis, let's do this!"

Where Do You Place Your Burden Basket

(1)

The old Lakota women gathered their firewood.
They gathered small sticks easy enough to pick up
and carry in their burden baskets.
Their hands were free to gather and carry,
which allowed them to be self-reliant.
They could then build their grandmother fires,
which burned hot with very little smoke,
and warm the evening lodge
without the smoke that could burn lungs.

The high school bully saw the younger man in a crowded bar.
He called him "faggot" in front of a hundred stunned people
who stopped everything to watch
as he slammed the much smaller man's head
four times against an empty table.
The young man thought,
in the middle of his totally passive response,
the silence in the room deafening,
"Better to not antagonize this noted hater,
or I might die."

When the hate-filled man released his grip,
the young man simply walked out of the bar,
his head throbbing.
Briefly he wondered why no one came to assist him.
He realized they probably all felt the same way,
that they too might die.
He decided to leave it to fate
that this guy would someday get his just rewards.

(2)

When the burden basket was not in use,
the Lakota women hung them outside their door.
In their tradition
they were not asked to bear a burden
heavier than their baskets could handle.
Placing them outside their entrance
reminded all guests
to "Leave his or her personal complaints or problems in the burden basket
before entering their personal space."
To "Enter another's home with a black cloud of worry
or neediness is considered very poor manners.
To be in the present moment,
and to be willing to be a welcome guest,
required strength of character.
To have compassion for the burdens of others,
and yet not take those burdens as their own,
required a strong heart."

The three drunks rear-ended and totaled
his uninsured clown car, his home.
As his partner lay crumpled in the middle of the 4-lane,
their few possessions scattered about the road,
his own body twisted and bruised from the impact,
he looked to see what had hit them from behind
that early cold morning.
He saw the car a few hundred yards away
in a tangle of trees and earth and metal.
They needed the jaws of life
to separate those in that car from the fractured and twisted shards.
He couldn't bring himself to sue them.
He felt sorry for them.
He believed their road would be a difficult one
and didn't want to add to their heavy burden.
He hoped God would take care of them and him wisely.

(3)

For many native peoples
the burden basket is a symbol
of the "Internal strength necessary
to keep one's own counsel and bear one's own burdens
without inflicting them on others."
They believe the burden basket
teaches, "Trust to value our own answers
through our connection to great mystery and the medicine helpers."

He woke with the woman touching him:
without permission touching him.
She knew he was gay.
She knew he was not interested in her.
She had tricked him with her hidden agenda,
and he erupted into a tirade at her.
He pulled out the well maintained and intricate mental list
of all her recorded wrongs, abuses, and faulty character traits.
He barraged her with the soul wounding that he felt,
left her crying in a heap,
wailing outside his window deep into the night to forgive her.
But he couldn't then.
He ran from place to place and person to person,
seeking help, advice, healing,
bad mouthing her and all her attempts
to say he had spurred her on,
until he lapsed into a deep depression.
He asked karma to help heal her and himself.

(4)

The native's burden basket advised them
to only carry the burdens they wished to carry.
And if it made one "Feel good or important
to have so much to handle,
then one might need to look at the idea of self-importance."
If one needed help and advice

it was best to then approach a healer
or medicine person with reverence
and to honor their sacred advice to the letter.

When the old psychiatrist told him after his first few sessions
that he was doomed to wander aimlessly and without hope
because he had no one foundation of belief from which to operate,
that there was nothing of stability to support him,
he was at first angry.
He quit that man right away.

After many years he woke up,
prayed to the seven directions
beyond time and space,
chanted his reiki healing sounds into his sore spaces,
did some yoga to loosen his multileveled restrictions,
and chopped some firewood for his sacred faery sweat lodge.
He thanked Mary, Jesus, Buddha, No Shate', his bear guide,
Tanka Shila, the ever-changing mystery,
Ganesha, and a host of other guides,
and then laughed deeply into his burden basket—
like Jesus feeding loaves and fishes to the starving.

Note: *information and quotations in each first stanza of each section are from "The Sacred Path" divination deck by Jamie Sams.

Just Walking My Path

I met Jesus in Provincetown, Massachusetts one day.
As I gave Reiki to my friend, I had a vision
in which he appeared walking down a dirt road.
As I watched him from 10 yards away,
Jesus suddenly turned toward me.
He looked straight into my eyes.
A ray of bright, emerald green light busted forth from his heart
and sped toward me, silently piercing the veils into my heart.
The 6 inches-wide ray of green light flowed unwavering,
connecting our bodies together.
I felt a bliss in my being that I had never felt before.
The woman under my hands had yipped
as it entered both me and her at the exact same time,
and tears welled in her eyes.
When the session finished
she told me she felt happy and had a profound lightness in her being.
I relayed my experience to her.
She accepted it all with a broad smile
and a shake of her head in affirmation.
Dumbfounded and awe filled, I was humbled.
I had always wanted and prayed to heal the way Jesus had healed
even though I had left the church system long before.

I met Gurumayi Chidvilasananda in Provincetown one night.
As I slept with my partner,
I dreamed I was lying beside him
in a different bed in a different room.
I awoke in the dream to see a boyish, youthful person
standing at the foot of the bed against the wall.
He had a close-shaved head.
In the dream I asked aloud,
"Who is this?"
I heard a response that said, "It is your next lover!"
I awoke with a gasp and a feeling of confusion.

A week later I saw a picture of Gurumayi for the first time.
She was a renunciate with a close shaved head
and was taking on the mantle of her teacher Muktananda.
Confused, I began to listen to her talks and chants
and planned to visit her ashram.

I met Muktananda at Gurumayi's ashram in New York one day.
He danced on my head like a squirrel
in a meditation designed to meet him led by Gurumayi.
He tippy-tapped his tiny feet in rapid succession on my crown
and chittered news at me.
He ran down my leg and back up it three times,
dancing excitedly and holding Sat Sang each time
even though it did not register to me that it was him at first.
Finally I understood that I needed to settle my mind
and pay attention.
Baba Muktananda helped me to release some body-held, ages-old grief
through several meditations.
One time I sobbed uncontrollably for several hours into my own lap,
not even knowing what I was crying about,
until my pants and shirt were sopped with tears of liberation.

I met Noshate', my bear guide, on Zuni Mountain, New Mexico.
She came to me in a dream, threatening to bite my head off.
She raked her claws against my left arm,
almost seeming to pull it off, as I awoke startled.
She came the next night, and the same dream occurred.
She came a third night, but this time
she wrapped her huge mouth over my cantankerous neighbor's head.
On this third visit I suddenly recognized the bear as my guide
and somehow knew that she was trying to tell me
to shut off my yakking mind-talk.
I decided to call her in to let her dismantle
and psychically reassemble me in a shamanic redo.
In deep trance drum journey
I witnessed, without pain or gore,
Noshate' take off my head to place an eagle's head there.

Then she pulled out my human heart to give me an elk's heart.
Then a wolf's left arm and a badger's right arm joined to me.
And finally, two bear legs and a buffalo horn penis
were re-membered to me.
It has been years of trying to understand
that exchange and its meanings.

I met a sabre tooth tiger along the Pecos River, New Mexico
through an ancient tooth I wore with pride around my neck.
The tiger leapt with me one day
into the bottom of the Lakota Sundance pit
where the sacred pole would soon be placed.
She and I clawed with my hands
to consecrate the walls of the sacred womb,
dredging ancestral memories and the potential of the earth
with our conjoined anger at children being molested.
She anointed the hole with my sacred tears of grief
that poured into the barren, high desert, arid soil.
We prayed together for all the abused children of the world.
She left my awareness, and I climbed out of the Sundance pit
to receive the thanks
of a huge, etheric buffalo standing in the west gate,
his hot belching breath snorting against my face.
Even though he physically was not there,
I felt the wave of his heat and emotion.
I saw and heard and felt him paw the ground,
and I knew it was in thanks.
I knew it would be a good dance that year with blessings abounding.

I met a consciousness that cared for me one day
as I lay in my cabana on the Southern-most point
of the Big Island of Hawaii.
My heart had been racing with images of the tsunami
that had just crushed Indonesia two days before,
which brought a vivid memory to me
of a tsunami demolishing Hilo in the 1950's.
I saw the wall of water come up from the ocean
to swamp and kill whomever's eyes I looked through.

My mind had been racing
from someone aggressively trespassing my sexual boundaries
a few hours earlier.
My inner child screamed from under bars of terror
that had been smothered behind 25 years of cigarette smoke,
which I had just stopped a few weeks earlier.
My mother had just died 4 months prior,
and my soul body trembled like Kilauea Volcano,
which was erupting just a mile away
and shaking the ground and stinking the air up with sulfur.
Suddenly my hands and feet were lifted up from the bed
as if someone invisible were picking me up.
Only my butt rested on the bed as I struggled to free myself,
my legs and arms upraised toward the ceiling.
I felt like I was hog-tied.
I tried to scream, but couldn't.
Tears streamed down my face.

I knew it was something old in my body,
something my inner child was now internally screaming about.
I heard someone inside me say, "It's okay. You are safe."
I heard them say it three times.
I let go of the struggle in my arms and legs.
They just remained uplifted into the air.
I felt a cupping under me
as if a giant hand held me up
and comforted and protected me.
I relaxed into the hands
and stayed that way for a long enough time.
Then my body released gently to me, lying flat.
I curled on my side and wept again,
this time for joy.
Another new comfort in the ever-changing mystery.

I thank all the many guides that have come to help
and to guide me through the years.
Through dreams, visions, and meditations
you have led me back to peace and love.

Blessed be!

RedWulf DancingBare

In search of what would make his heart sing, RedWulf DancingBare (Ralph Greco) traversed the country in search of meaning. At 50, he found the Zuni Mountain Poets and began to scribe his story. His writings reflect his time spent as a closeted gay youth who now calls himself a "two spirit." He often danced with the Lakota's as a Winkte' in Sun Dance and also stewarded a Radical Faerie Sanctuary. His poetry draws upon many diverse experiences that reflect his time spent as a circus clown, United Unitarian (U.U.) lay minister, chef, massage therapist, and potter, among other work, and exemplify his present chosen identities as Reiki master/psychic counselor, baker/café manager, and photographer/poet.

www.ingramcontent.com/pod-product-compliance
Lightning Source LLC
Chambersburg PA
CBHW070733020526
44118CB00035B/1227